ADVANCES IN
COLLECTION DEVELOPMENT AND
RESOURCE MANAGEMENT

Volume 1 • 1995

ADVANCES IN COLLECTION DEVELOPMENT AND RESOURCE MANAGEMENT

Editor: THOMAS W. LEONHARDT
University of Oklahoma

VOLUME 1 • 1995

 JAI PRESS INC.

Greenwich, Connecticut   *London, England*

CONTENTS

LIST OF CONTRIBUTORS

J. Michael Alford

Business Administration
The Citadel

Mary Bushing

Collection Development
Montana State University

William Fisher

School of Library and
   Information Science
San Jose State University

Margaret Henty

Conspectus Officer
National Library of Australia

William C. Highfill

University Libraries
Auburn University

Thomas W. Leonhardt

Library Technical Services
Collection Development
University of Oklahoma

Sue O. Medina

Network of Alabama Academic
   Libraries

Elaine Peterson

Technical Services
Montana State University

Cecilia Schmitz

University Libraries
Auburn University

T. Harmon Straiton, Jr.

Microforms and Documents
   Department
Auburn University

A. Bruce Strauch

Law and Economics
The Citadel

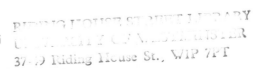

INTRODUCTION

This inaugural of what we hope becomes an annual, took shape slowly. Although the title of the series, *Advances in Collection Development and Resource Management*, covers most of what we do in libraries, practitioners, no matter how well they write, often find it difficult to set aside the necessary time in order to chronicle the advances they make daily in their rapidly changing world.

One preferred method of sharing is by addressing colleagues at professional conferences. Even these speakers tend not to have publishable papers in front of them when they present their topics. This system works reasonably well as far as it goes but unless the papers are published, the audience remains small and the medium is transitory.

The papers in this volume were not delivered at conferences but were written for this publication by practitioners, for the most part, and for their efforts we thank them. Writing is a hard, thankless, and risky business.

The eight papers cover collection management, resource sharing, legal issues, and education. They are aimed primarily at practitioners but at the same time they are also useful for administrators, educators, and students.

Medina provides, through a bibliographical essay, a history of overlap studies. This should be required reading for anyone contemplating an overlap study, for whatever reason or use. This piece is a fine example of an alternative to the annotated bibliography that many of us find so useful.

Bushing and Peterson present a solid argument for weeding collections and tell us how to proceed with the presentation of a case study.

Medina, Straiton, and Schmitz provide a brief history of major microform sets and their bibliographic control. Most of the paper, however, is a case study of a statewide effort to identify, catalog, and publicize the substantial resources held in microform. That effort was the basis for a union list of Alabama holdings of major microform sets.

Another Alabama project resulted in the Network of Alabama Academic Libraries (NAAL). Medina and Highfill describe the history, purpose, and governance structure of NAAL and show that cooperative collection development can work if all parties and at the highest level can make a binding commitment.

Moving beyond the state level, Henty describes Australia's efforts to define a distributed national collection. In other words, what is mine is yours, what is yours is mine. Again, a key element for success was a high level commitment.

Strauch, a lawyer and college professor, advises librarians that the academic world may not be immune to challenges from those who would challenge some of the materials that are acquired for teaching and research.

Alford and Strauch remind us that we live in litigious times and that the handshake of a sales representative is not as binding as it once was.

Fisher walks the reader through some of the debates of the past quarter century on education for acquisitions librarians. His conclusion is that librarians will have to do for themselves what library schools cannot or will not do for them.

There are many issues in collection development and resource management that are not covered in this volume. We hope that in Volume 2 we will be able to address more of those issues such as organizational shifts, interlibrary lending and borrowing, preservation, and budgeting, to name just a few. There is a lot going on that we can share with each other.

Thomas W. Leonhardt
Editor

DUPLICATION AND OVERLAP AMONG LIBRARY COLLECTIONS
A CHRONOLOGICAL REVIEW OF THE LITERATURE

Sue O. Medina

Cooperation among libraries for resource sharing activities requires participants to examine the nature of their own collections as well as each collection's relationship to other collections. The need for collection management information to identify deficiencies, understand strengths and weaknesses, expand coverage, or reduce unnecessary redundancy has led to investigations of similarity among collections. Commonly called "overlap" studies, these seek to determine the level of diversity and similarity in titles held by two or more libraries. The resulting data are usually reported as percentages of titles held in common similarity, and/or diversity. The findings of overlap studies have implications for joint planning

Advances in Collection Development and Resource Management,
Volume 1, pages 1-60.
Copyright © 1995 by JAI Press Inc.
All rights of reproduction in any form reserved.
ISBN: 1-55938-213-9

for library services including (1) shared database development and union catalogs, (2) interlibrary loan, and (3) cooperative acquisitions, cataloging, storage, and collection development programs.

William Potter reviewed overlap studies in 1982 and classified them according to four purposes: studies related to union catalogs, studies related to centralized processing, studies for collection development, and research studies undertaken to further understanding of collections. He noted that studies concerned with union catalogs are intent on examining diversity while those concerned with centralized processing are interested in similarity.[1] Ten years later, Potter's categories are still useful. However, additional classifications are needed for studies undertaken to facilitate resource sharing which may occur in the absence of a union catalog, shared cataloging or technical processing center, or collection development. For example, three studies were undertaken to investigate or implement the merger of libraries. Many studies do not have a single purpose and may fall into more than one category.

The majority of the seventy-three overlap studies included in this chronological review were for libraries in the United States with fifty-six studies reported through 1993. This large number is followed by seven studies from Australia (two of these report different annual data for the same acquisitions program), three from the United Kingdom (all using the same source data), two from South Africa, and one each from Canada, Germany (Prussia), Great Britain, and Scotland. Two studies cross international borders, one examining overlap among public libraries in the United States and Canada and one reporting an early UNESCO project to test the feasibility of creating a union catalog for Europe from the catalogs of the national libraries.

Academic libraries were the principal concern of most researchers. Forty-six studies used data primarily from academic libraries which ranged in size from large research libraries to small college, including junior college, libraries. Twenty of these studies focused on research libraries with the definition of research library generally meaning large university libraries but often including national or state libraries. Fourteen studies involved more than one type of library. Of these, ten studied holdings from multiple types, usually a consortium of libraries within a close geographical area. Proximity seemed a factor in the studies involving school and public libraries (3 studies) and academic and public libraries (1 study). Few studies focused exclusively on school libraries (5 studies) or public libraries (3 studies). Several studies limited their analysis by subject, with special libraries the concern of six studies: four in the health sciences area and two for theological library consortia.

Higher education played an important role as stimulus for overlap research. Twelve studies were doctoral dissertations, and four were theses. The research methodology for these was rigorous and reported in detail. The methodology seemed no less rigorous for the other studies, but was less often described in detail. All of the studies conducted since 1975 owe a debt to William K. Buckland, Anthony Hindle, and Gregory P.M. Walker for their excellent discussion of the problems associated with overlap research.[2]

One of the earliest reports concerned with duplication among libraries was a brief mention by Herman Fussler in a 1940 presentation on the use of microfilm in libraries. He quoted an unpublished translation by Herbert Goldhor of an article on an overlap study done in Germany which stated:

> Copies of the book thus rapidly become rare and cannot be found a few years after publication.... [T]his situation has been confirmed by a statistical study recently made in Germany. The Royal Library of Berlin and eleven university libraries of Prussia, having agreed to establish a union catalog (the Gesamtkatalog), were disappointed in their hope of achieving great economy in their work, because it was found that 60 per cent of the titles were held by only one of the twelve libraries.[3]

Fussler did not discuss overlap beyond this brief comment, but his concern that older materials become rare as they age and are less likely to be duplicated appears in subsequent investigations of duplication.

The first American study undertaken specifically to examine overlap was published in 1942 by the Bibliographical Planning Committee of Philadelphia. It examined duplication in response to a grant awarded by the Carnegie Foundation for an experimental Bibliographic Center. As part of its extensive report on area libraries and services, the Committee noted that a "card-by-card comparison of the first eighty-seven trays of the Union Library Catalogue with the corresponding section of the Union Catalog at the Library of Congress has shown that about 36 percent of the items listed in the Union Library Catalogue represent material for which the national Union Catalog had no record."[4]

It is likely that the Philadelphia data were part of the first major American research of collection overlap which was completed to determine the number of books held by American libraries, determine the extent to which these had been duplicated in collections, and identify which libraries should potentially be included in the Library of Congress Union Catalog, later the National Union Catalog.[5] In October 1940, Leroy C. Merritt analyzed a sample of 3,682 titles for duplication among the 46 members of the Association of Research Libraries using records reported to the Library of Congress Union Catalog and 129 other library and union catalogs. Merritt paired data for each library with every other library and reported his findings as percentages in tables labeled "Index of Inclusiveness" and "Index of Duplication." The Index of Inclusiveness represented the extent to which each library included the same titles also held by other libraries in the group; these percentages for duplication ranged from 1.4 to 56.2 percent. The Index of Duplication represented the average extent to which the holdings of each library were *not* duplicated by any other library in the group; these percentages for uniqueness ranged from 9.8 to 36.1 percent. Additional analyses found positive correlations between size of the library measured by number of volumes held and a high percentage on the indices for "inclusiveness" and "duplication." Merritt concluded that "In general, then, it is possible to say that the larger a library is in terms of the volumes it holds, the more apt it is to include the holdings of other libraries, and the more apt it is to own works that other libraries have not acquired."[6] In addition to noting the linear relationship between size and level of duplication, Merritt suggested that a policy of library cooperation could make it possible to reduce duplication and acquire titles not available in any of the libraries' collections.

For his dissertation, Andrew Eaton researched coverage and duplication among five Chicago research libraries for 1937 imprints of book trade publications in political science for five countries (United States, England, France, Germany, and Italy). The Chicago libraries held 621 or 46 percent of the 1,338 books on his checklist.

The majority, 71 percent, of the books held were in English and most had been published in the United States. Also, 59 percent of the titles held by the Chicago libraries were held by two or more of them. For comparison purposes, he examined coverage in the New York Public Library and found 66 percent of the titles in the sample. Eaton called for a broad program of coordinated acquisitions by the Chicago area libraries to eliminate unnecessary duplication, to correct gaps in coverage, and to achieve adequate coverage in important subject fields.[7]

The inability of the Library of Congress to provide printed cards for more than fifty percent of the materials acquired by Columbia University challenged Catherine C. Blodgett to study duplication in original cataloging. Her thesis examined the feasibility of cooperative cataloging by collecting data on original cataloging done by six research libraries in the New York City area. She drew a sample of 500 titles cataloged by Columbia University and determined which of the titles were held by New York Public Library and five universities offering graduate study. She excluded serials and book titles not likely to be held by each of the academic institutions (for example, titles from the Schools of Law and Medicine and in the subjects of engineering and library science because not all of the universities offered these programs) and insured that the sample titles were distributed across a variety of subjects, formats, time periods, and languages. Columbia University and New York Public Library had the highest rate of duplication, slightly less than 20 percent. Columbia's rate of duplication with the other academic institutions in the study was low: Yale, 17.2 percent; Princeton, 13 percent; and New York University and Fordham each less than 3 percent. The highest levels of duplication occurred in history, literature, and social sciences materials, book format materials, titles published in English, and titles published during the period 1940-1946. Blodgett concluded that her findings did not support a recommendation for cooperative cataloging among the libraries but suggested that there might be a basis for cooperation in acquisitions.[8]

One consistent purpose for overlap studies has been to investigate the feasibility of establishing cooperative cataloging or processing centers. In the first of several such studies, John Minto Dawson examined cataloging data for current acquisitions to determine feasibility for centralized cataloging. He hypothesized that research libraries acquire a substantial proportion of material in common within a limited period of time. Nine large university libraries provided a catalog card for monographs cataloged during a two-week period. The resultant 5,142 titles were analyzed for acquisitions patterns. Only 182 titles were cataloged by two libraries, 23 by three libraries, and 4 by four libraries. Because of the short sample period, Dawson later drew a random sample of 250 titles from his original sample and found that 82 percent of the titles were held by two or more of the nine libraries. As a result, Dawson concluded that, over time, university libraries tend to acquire titles in common.[9]

In an article published in 1958, Theodore Besterman described a post-World War II need for union catalogs throughout the world and reviewed UNESCO efforts to test the feasibility of developing a union catalog for Europe. The background information reviewing national catalogs and union catalog initiatives included reports on overlap. No sources for the data were given and the collection and analysis of data may have been done by Besterman for the UNESCO project. He stated that unique copies comprised 84 percent of the entries in a small union catalog of entries for twenty Swiss libraries. Besterman compared 2,293 entries (Abe-Aberdeen) from the U.S. National Union Catalog to entries for the same alphabetical range in three European catalogs: the British Museum catalog, Biblioteque Nationale catalog, and Deutscher Gesamtkatalog. The three European catalogs contained only 1,652 entries for this range. He also reported that 73 percent of the entries in the American catalog were not in the European catalogs and that 63 percent of the European entries were not in the American union catalog. Of the 1,652 entries from the European catalogs, only 60 were duplicated between the British Museum and the Biblioteque Nationale while only 65 duplicates were found for the Biblioteque Nationale and the Deutscher Gesamtkatalog. Only 29 entries were found in all three European catalogs. UNESCO funded a pilot European catalog project for six months in 1947. In the absence of an international cataloging code, Besterman quickly compiled a code and invited catalogers to submit cataloging records to a union catalog. The project actually operated for only three months and received 73,000 cards. During this short period only 19,809 entries were filed and analyzed, of which 17,769 or 89.7 percent were reported by only one library. In another analysis of the first 7,947 cards filed, there were 2,413 French books, of which 2,104 or 87.1 percent were reported by only one library; and 1,898 German books, of which 1,568 or 82.6 percent were reported by only one library. The problems of cataloging without an international code, disruption and destruction caused by World War II, differences in national publishing output and distribution, and differences in languages for both publications and catalogers give Besterman's data little influence in planning international cooperative programs in today's world. However, the UNESCO effort is an interesting foundation in the history of overlap studies.[10]

The Council of Higher Educational Institutions charged Ruth Estes with studying the resources, facilities, and use of seven private college and university libraries in the downtown Brooklyn area. The Council hoped that her recommendations would lead to more effective use of library funds to enhance library service. As part of her research, she examined overlap of current acquisitions and periodical subscriptions. A sample of 279 general titles recently acquired by Pratt Institute was checked against the holdings of the six other colleges. No specialized materials were included in the sample. The rate of duplication ranged from no overlap to 59 titles in literature and philosophy (100 titles). In science (79 titles) overlap ranged from none to 59 titles, and in social sciences (100 titles) it ranged from 3 to 90 titles. Estes found substantial duplication among the general titles examined but indicated that some was inevitable to support duplicated teaching areas. Her findings of 90 percent duplication in social sciences (Pratt and Long Island University) and 80 percent duplication in science (Pratt and Polytechnic Institute) suggested further study to improve the investment of book funds and joint use of purchased materials. She based her analysis of duplication of periodicals on a union list of serials which did not include titles with subscriptions at three or more libraries. In spite of this limitation, she found that over half of the titles were duplicated at least once (45% of the titles were uniquely held). She recommended formal agreements to designate which library should subscribe to selected titles with ready access provided to the other libraries through interlibrary loan and to students through direct admission to the owning library. To facilitate resource sharing, she suggested that the union list include all subscriptions and that it be updated to insure currency.[11]

Everett Moore reported the level of duplication in acquisitions as part of his investigation into the feasibility of establishing a cataloging and processing center for a group of public junior colleges in southern California. Twenty libraries responded to his request to check their holdings on a list of 100 titles sampled from *Choice*. He found 99 titles representing 828 volumes were owned. While the study findings were not reported as percentages for duplicate or unique items, the rate of duplication can be derived as 8.36 volumes per title. Moore concluded that the junior colleges did acquire materials at a sufficient rate of duplication (at least five copies of each title among the thirty-five possible participants) to justify the establishment of a shared center for cataloging and processing.[12]

Marilyn Stahle analyzed current cataloging data to investigate the feasibility of developing a cooperative acquisitions program among eight academic and research libraries in the Greater Boston Area. She collected approximately 40,000 main entry cards for titles with 1960-1963 imprints cataloged by each library from July 1962 to July 1963, with the exception of acquisitions in four special collections. The study was limited by the speed with which each library acquired and cataloged individual titles. The findings were also restricted by its limitation to titles cataloged in one year rather than acquisitions for the year or all titles with a given imprint date. To develop a manageable working sample, Stahle excluded serials, internal duplicates, and pre-1960 imprints from the entries and then extracted every tenth title and all cards representing that title. Several analyses were completed using this smaller sample including number of acquisitions by each library; distribution of acquisitions among the libraries and by subject, foreign languages, and publication date; and variations in speed with which materials were acquired and cataloged. To examine duplication, the sample was further restricted to only 1962 imprints. These 1,063 titles represented 1,880 volumes; 609 titles or 57.2 percent were uniquely held. There was little duplication of the 31 foreign titles in the sample with 29 titles uniquely held. Stahle analyzed overlap between pairs of libraries in selected subjects and displayed the findings in several tables. The highest level of unique holdings (75%) was for titles in LC classification G at Boston Public Library followed by the technology classification at Massachusetts Institution of Technology (70% unique) and Boston Public (69.2% unique), the philosophy collection (LC class B) at Boston University (57.1% unique), and the medical collection (LC class R) at Tufts University (56.7% unique). Titles held by some of the smaller libraries in the selected subjects were completely duplicated within the group. Among her findings, Stahle noted that duplication decreases as the number of acquisitions increases.[13]

William R. Nugent studied the extent of duplication among six New England state universities in order to estimate the efficiency of a proposed reclassification project and to predict the degree of joint use of cataloging information. His findings were presented as levels of duplication between ordered pairs of libraries for both the entire sample from the general collection and for a subset of current imprints. The overlap percentages for the general collection ranged from 28.1 percent to 55.2 percent and had an average of 39.7 percent. Duplication for the current imprint sample had a greater range, 25.1 percent to 70.6 percent, and a higher average, 46.9 percent. Nugent reported that the percentage (which he called probabilities) of duplication in each of the libraries appeared directly related to library size, but with less variation than size alone would cause.[14]

Ralph Parker examined duplication among the collections of five university libraries in metropolitan Washington, D.C. to determine the feasibility of a jointly-owned computerized processing center. He checked a sample of 200 titles, excluding serials, acquired by each library during a two-year period. Imprint dates for these "current acquisitions" varied from 1941 to 1967. This nonserial sample was checked in the catalogs of the five libraries and the results displayed as the percentage of duplication between each pair of libraries. Duplication rates ranged from 35 to 77 percent with 61.5 percent of the titles duplicated at least once in the five university libraries. Of the 200 titles in this sample, 77 were uniquely held. In a similar analysis of 200 currently-received serials titles, Parker found less duplication, 119 titles or 59.5 percent were unique.[15] Buckland, Hindle, and Walker in their review of the methodological problems in overlap studies, stated that Parker's approach using a single undifferentiated sample from the nonproportionate samples taken from each of the five libraries studied is statistically improper.[16]

In the first of two studies to use samples drawn from the *American Book Publishing Record*, Lawrence C. Leonard, Joan M. Maier, and Richard M. Dougherty examined the feasibility of a centralized processing center for nine Colorado academic libraries. The researchers calculated a table of probabilities using data from checking holdings of a sample of 1,208 titles to forecast the expected number of duplicate copies that would be ordered within the system. Their reported probabilities ranged from 4 percent to 70 percent and reflected the percentages of duplication found between pairs of libraries.[17]

One of the first duplication studies undertaken specifically in the context of a formal cooperative collection development program assessed the effectiveness of an acquisitions agreement among libraries in New South Wales, Australia. In the mid-1960s, the New South Wales Book Resources Committee established a plan for cooperative acquisitions. The libraries first completed statements of their practice and intent in regard to collecting in depth. A preliminary survey of holdings of publications originating in designated geographical areas indicated that the libraries could effectively cooperate to collect all significant publications from various geographic regions. Accordingly, in 1968, the Library of New South Wales and five university libraries accepted geographic responsibilities and agreed to collect at the reference level for their assigned area. Without additional funds for the scheme, responsibility was limited to currently published materials including official publications, statistics, and serials. Participants might acquire retrospective materials but these were not given priority. In 1968, Harrison Bryan surveyed the participating libraries to determine the extent of coverage and duplication. He found that the short period of time in which the scheme had been operating was not sufficient to demonstrate substantial increases in coverage. The libraries identified 936 items as part of the scheme of which 357 or 38.1 percent were unique. In 1969, a list from each library was checked against the holdings of all other participants. A total of 1,338 items was reported (an increase of almost 50 percent over 1968). Of these, 552 or 41.3 percent were uniquely held. In an array of paired libraries, duplication ranged from 4.3 percent to 70.3 percent. The number of items duplicated by each library of the total items selected by all libraries ranged from 13.2 percent to 51.7 percent. Bryan concluded that the two largest libraries duplicated the most but also contributed the highest proportion of unique items. The two larger libraries also accounted overwhelmingly for duplication of the more expensive items. In a comparison with teaching programs, the data linked duplication of library materials to overlap in teaching among the universities. These findings supported the Committee's contention that there was very little unnecessary duplication among library collections.[18] In another article, Bryan examined subsequent acquisitions and holdings of the 1969 imprints and examined holdings of 1970 imprints.[19] Results of this study are reported later in this chronological review.

Another Australian study was also undertaken specifically in the context of cooperative collection development. It relied on holdings reported to the Union Catalogue of Serials and the Outlier Union Catalogue (monographs) to determine the extent of duplication among the Library Board of Western Australia, the University of Western Australia, and the Western Australian Institute of Technology. Ursula De Vaz and Lennie McCall drew a random sample of 604 serial titles from the union list of serials and found 38 titles duplicated by at least two of the libraries. Subject librarians, asked to determine which titles they would likely discontinue knowing that duplication existed, indicated that only two titles (both received gratis) were not necessary in their libraries. For monographs, a random sample of titles cataloged in science and technology (Dewey 500-600) with 1968 imprints was drawn from the printed subject catalog containing holdings of the State Reference Library and the circulating collection of the Library Board. This sample of 208 titles was checked against the holdings contributed to the Outlier Union Catalog with 45 titles reported held by one or both of the university libraries. When asked about eliminating duplicated titles, librarians indicated that only two titles would not have been acquired. De Vaz and McCall concluded that there was no significant duplication of serials or monographs. They noted that no formal method for coordination of book selection would be needed because the cost would likely exceed any savings.[20]

In the late 1960s and early 1970s, the Library Research Unit of
the University of Lancaster prepared two studies for the National
Libraries ADP Study. The *National Catalogue Coverage Study*
described the methodology used to develop the sample for both
studies. The edited proportionate sample constituted about 23,000
items held within a group of eighteen research libraries which
represented all "national" and copyright deposit libraries as well as
a selection of other research libraries in the United Kingdom. From
this main sample, appropriate subsamples were drawn to check
holdings. Subsample sizes checked in individual research library
catalogs ranged from 92 items for the Science Museum Library
(about 90,000 volumes) to 942 items for the British Museum (about
2.8 million volumes).

The *National Catalogue Coverage Study* examined overlap of
monographs within the group of eighteen research libraries. Three
additional analyses were made: overlap of five special libraries with
the research libraries, the extent to which holdings of individual
libraries were represented in union catalogs of the National Central
Library and in the printed cards of the Library of Congress, and
overlap of pre-1920 holdings in the Bodleian Library, Oxford
University, with the research libraries' holdings. Conclusions related
to overlap were not discussed in the report but the data were reported
as percentages and arrayed in a table which paired each research
library with every other research library. Given the wide variety of
libraries in the study, the range of percentages was extensive with
several libraries demonstrating no or little overlap. The highest rate
of overlap, 80.93 percent, was between the British Museum (the
largest with about 2.8 million volumes) and the National Library of
Scotland (the fourth largest with 1.2 million volumes). Data for the
special libraries were presented as a proportion of material in the
special libraries which was not held by the group of research libraries.
Findings for uniquely held materials ranged from 4 percent of the
materials held by the University of Aston, a science and technology
collection, to 50 percent of the holdings of the Slavonic Library,
Cambridge University. One key result of the study was the estimate
that the libraries of Great Britain held 4.5 to 4.75 million different
monographs. Completeness of coverage in union catalogs varied
widely with 21 percent of the British Museum's books but 70 percent

of the University of Lancaster holdings represented in the union catalogs of the National Central Library. For most of the research libraries examined, 30 to 50 percent of their holdings were represented by Library of Congress printed cards. The study of Bodleian holdings was undertaken because of ongoing work to convert the catalog of pre-1920 imprints to machine-readable format. Overlap of Bodleian pre-1920 holdings with each of the eighteen research libraries ranged from .99 percent with the School of Oriental and African Studies, University of London, to 64.53 percent with the British Museum. Overlap of pre-1920 holdings of the research libraries with the Bodleian library ranged from 29.89 percent with the Royal Society of Medicine to 67.89 percent with the National Library of Scotland. In a comparison with the entire group of research libraries, 24.63 percent of the pre-1920 imprints were held uniquely by the Bodleian.[21]

The *Foreign Books Acquisitions Study* examined the extent of duplication of modern foreign books within the group of research libraries. A sample of titles selected from the catalogs of the libraries, excluding non-European languages, was checked. This analysis found that 56 percent of the titles were held uniquely. The overall rate of duplication was 2.1 copies per title. The rate of duplication for foreign-imprint, English-language titles with 1950-1967 imprint dates was 2.8 copies per title with 47 percent of the titles held uniquely. Non-English language, 1950-1967 imprint dates, foreign imprints had a duplication rate of 1.7 copies per title with 62 percent of the titles held uniquely.[22]

The possibility of expanding coverage and the level of acquisitions among four research libraries in the Pittsburgh area of currently reviewed and recommended materials in business and economics was the focus of research by John DePew. Using authoritative review journals he developed a sample of 1,291 titles which had been recommended as necessary to a core collection. The four libraries held 1,143 titles or 88.54 percent of the sample; none held 11.6 percent of the titles. The rate of duplication for the 1,143 titles held was 77.78 percent with 254 titles or 22.2 percent held by only one library. DePew noted that some titles which should have been acquired had not been and recommended that the libraries institute acquisitions procedures based on systematic and accurate study to acquire what is needed as it becomes available. Further, noting the high rate of duplication and the omission of titles which should have been acquired by the Pittsburgh libraries, he recommended coordination of acquisitions to ensure that important materials are acquired and duplication kept to a minimum.[23]

Ellen Altman used an overlap study to assess the feasibility of establishing an interlibrary loan program among school libraries in New Jersey. A sample drawn from thirty-one schools and four area public libraries provided 6,698 titles representing 22,557 volumes (a ratio of 1 to 3.37) in twelve topical subjects. School libraries owned 3,498 titles (52.5% of the sample) representing 12,829 volumes. Public libraries owned 5,595 titles (83.5%) representing 9,728 volumes. The school and public libraries collectively held 35.77 percent of the titles. Titles held only by school libraries represented 16.4 percent of the sample and 47.7 percent of the titles were held only by public libraries. The sample titles were checked in *Standard Catalog for High School Libraries* (8th ed.) and its successor the *Senior High School Library Catalog* (9th ed.) to determine holdings and overlap for "core" materials. On the average, the school libraries collectively held 11 volumes for each title listed in the bibliographies (core) but only 2.73 volumes for titles not listed (noncore). Unique titles represented 48.1 percent of the noncore titles in the collective school holdings. The holdings of unique titles in individual school collections ranged from 10.2 to 37.2 percent. No correlation was found between the percentage of unique titles and the total size of a school's noncore collection. One significant finding that 31.4 percent or 12,829 volumes of the total 22,557 volumes representing the sample titles were held only by school libraries implied that school libraries could supply titles through interlibrary loan which were not available in the area public libraries. Thus, Altman concluded that even the smallest libraries would contribute to an interlibrary loan network and that all participants would gain by cooperation. Like other studies examining the linear relationship between size and unique holdings, this study also found that the relationship of unique titles to total holdings was proportionate. No school library would contribute an inordinate proportion of unique titles to the collective holdings, in terms of absolute numbers; however, the number of unique titles was greater in larger collections. As part of her research, Altman also developed a frequency distribution model for the design of an optimum system.[24]

In 1972, Harrison Bryan reported on an additional analysis of the 1969 acquisitions data along with an analysis of 1970 acquisitions data for the New South Wales Area Collecting Scheme which had begun in 1968. The 1969 list was checked against the National Union Catalogue of Monographs which revealed more holdings than had been reported in his first analysis. This increase was attributed to normal time lag in acquiring and cataloging materials. Of the 1,311 monographs from the original title list checked in the union catalog, 268 items or 20.3 were unique. The percentage of unique items held by individual libraries ranged from 8.1 to 32.5 percent. The number of items acquired in 1970 declined to 1,142, reflecting decreased purchasing power of the six universities. The rate of duplication fell from the initial 58.7 percent for the 1969 list to 57.4 percent for titles acquired in 1970. Checking the holdings of a seventh university that was not an original participant in the agreement increased duplication for the 1970 imprints to 65.1 percent. In every pair, except in two cases where the increase was marginal, the rate of duplication was reduced from the previous year. The percent of unique items ranged from 13.9 to 51.9 percent. Bryan concluded from this finding that the cooperative acquisitions agreement was working to increase coverage and reduce duplication. He stressed that while the goal of the program to extend coverage as economically as possible, some duplication is unavoidable.[25]

William E. McGrath and Donald J. Simon studied overlap using the Louisiana Numerical Register, a union catalog representing current acquisitions data contributed by 14 academic libraries, one public library, and the Louisiana State Library. An analysis of entries made over an 18-month period was used to model the expected distribution of titles among libraries. They found that 66 percent of the total volumes in the latest cumulation were unique; 34 percent of the volumes represented duplicates. Although the study could not account for libraries cataloging the same title outside the study period, the model derived from the study predicted a linear relationship between rate of duplication and size of library and a low degree of duplication among the participating libraries.[26]

Edward T. O'Neill surveyed the library resources for the Western New York Library Resources Council as part of a feasibility study for a computerized catalog serving public and academic libraries in the region. Eighteen research libraries, which included fifteen academic libraries, one large public library, and two special libraries, participated in the overlap study. The card catalogs of the libraries were checked for their holdings of 8,858 monographs selected by cluster sampling. He found an estimated overlap of 1.77 copies held for each title and concluded that approximately 56.4 percent of the total number of monographs in the region were unique. In addition to reporting findings for common holdings, O'Neill presented tables with data for the age of holdings and for common holdings in seventeen subject fields.[27]

An evaluation of the need for a centralized acquisitions and cataloging system for the University of London libraries measured duplication in current acquisitions over a period of six months. The data were examined at the end of the first and sixth months. Overlap at the end of the first month was very small; 94.5 percent of the orders were for unique items. Overlap increased but remained small after six months; 85.4 percent of the orders were for unique items. The researchers predicted that 77.3 percent of the orders over a twelve-month period would be for unique items with overlap unlikely to exceed 1.5 entries per title. They concluded that the data failed to support the need for a centralized system.[28]

Like the American research by Altman and by McGrath and Simon, research in England by W. Y. Arms sought to develop a mathematical model which might predict duplication in a union catalog. Arms conceptualized that such a model could be used to determine which libraries should be added to a union catalog. He used data from the National Libraries ADP study done by the University of Lancaster which assessed overlap among eighteen national and research libraries in the United Kingdom. Arms identified two problems in the selection of the sample which he attempted to correct mathematically to eliminate bias. First, five of the libraries included in the study were copyright libraries and received a depository copy of every British book published. Second, the selection of titles from each participating library catalog tended to favor the selection of a duplicated title over a unique title. Arms compared the results of using the model to actual data for several years of additions to the Union Catalogue of Books, in which 45 percent of the titles added had been uniquely held. The model and the actual data were comparable. The application of the model suggested that duplication in a union catalog could be avoided by selecting participants for their unique collections based on age and subject specialization or type of library rather than size. Further, Arms noted that for a homogeneous group of libraries the proportion of unique titles gained by additional entries would be small.[29]

In the second study to use a sample drawn from *American Book Publishing Record,* John Knightly researched collection overlap in relation to nineteen academic programs offered by twenty-two state-supported college and university libraries in Texas. In all nineteen programs, collection overlap was extensive; but each library collection contributed unique titles to the statewide resources. Collectively, the libraries held 92 percent of the titles in the sample; 91 percent of these titles were duplicated one or more times among the twenty-two libraries. Duplication between pairs of libraries averaged 52.3 percent and ranged from 45.6 to 64 percent. In all nineteen program areas, there was a pronounced tendency for holdings and duplication to rise progressively with the level of degree offered. The highest average rate of duplication was among those schools offering doctoral level programs (76%). Duplication decreased with the level of degree (master's, 56%; bachelors, 47%) and with no degree, 37 percent. Knightly noted that at the doctoral level, libraries acquired 61 percent of all the books classified in the subject and duplicated among themselves 76 percent of these acquisitions. He speculated that some of the duplication could be due to each library acquiring a large proportion of a finite number of publications in the subject. A subset of 114 titles reviewed in *Choice* was also analyzed for duplication. These titles were duplicated at a higher rate (11.2%) than titles not reviewed (7.8%). An additional analysis of duplication by subject did not reveal extensive differences among the sciences, social sciences, or humanities.[30]

A plan to establish a cooperative bibliographic center in Indiana included an overlap study by Galen Rike to determine the availability of records for current cataloging by Indiana libraries in the OCLC database. A sample of 1,590 current monographic records was searched; 369 or 25 percent were not found in the OCLC database. Results by type of library indicated that 61 or 17 percent of 357 records from three public libraries were unique, 172 or 28 percent of 619 records from five academic libraries were unique, 53 or 20 percent of 269 records from four school libraries were unique, and 43 or 25 percent of 170 records from ten special libraries were unique. While not a traditional overlap study comparing duplication within a small set of libraries, this study estimated the rate at which records might be found on OCLC in order to advance plans for OCLC cataloging services to be offered to Indiana libraries.[31] In interpreting the results, Barbara Markuson stated that the major surprise of the study was the high proportion of school library records for which OCLC records existed. She noted that this could have resulted from the sample including a large proportion of replacement titles (classic materials and replacements for older works) which were well represented in the OCLC database.[32]

In the early 1970s, Gale Sypher Jacob used the collection of six high schools to compile a classified bibliography for high school libraries which was subsequently incorporated into *Books for Secondary School Libraries*. Several factors determined the selection of the schools, including excellence of collection and library faculty, geographic diversity, curriculum, and community characteristics. One interesting aspect of the study was its use of a model designed by Ellen Altman which predicted that six libraries would collectively hold 105,790 titles of which 69,702 or 65 percent would be unique. The actual database prepared from the catalogs of each school was restricted to titles still in print; it included 85,197 books of which 52,000 or 61 percent were unique. Two samples representing titles in specific subjects were also analyzed for overlap: sociology (Dewey 301.4) and science (Dewey 550, 551, 551.4, 551.5). In sociology, there were 374 unique titles in 571 sample titles. Data for the science sample were given for each classification number: 25 unique titles of 39 classed in Dewey 550, 49 unique titles of 82 classed in Dewey 551, 87 unique titles of 146 classed Dewey 551.4, and 52 unique titles of 94 titles classed Dewey 551.5. Jacob did not provide percentages for uniqueness, but these can be derived: sociology, 65.5 percent, and science, 59 percent with the four classes ranging from 55 to 64 percent.[33]

The Victoria Commission of Colleges (Australia) commissioned research to examine the potential for cooperative development of the library services among its fourteen colleges offering advanced degrees. Duplication of monographs was investigated to assist in defining possible areas for cooperation. For the analysis, a sample was developed which represented the proportion of main entries belonging to each letter of the alphabet based on five years of Library of Congress cataloging (*Cumulation*, 1963-67). Sample clusters using ranges of the alphabet for main entries were identified and each library supplied photocopies of its main entries falling in each cluster. Collection sizes ranged from 77,448 volumes at the Royal Melbourne Institute of Technology to 5,479 volumes at the College of Nursing, Australia. Sample sizes ranged from 658 from the Royal Melbourne Institute of Technology to 53 from the Victorian College of Pharmacy (9,650 volumes). The total sample of 3,393 records included 1,808 unique records representing 53.29 percent of the total. Percent of unique holdings in each library ranged from 10.5 percent (11 of 105 entries) supplied by the Warrnambool Institute of Advanced Education to 72.3 percent (47 of 65 entries) provided by the College of Nursing, Australia. In a comparison between pairs of libraries, overlap ranged from none to 55.238 percent between the Warrnambool Institute of Advanced Education and the Swinburne College of Technology. The samples from two libraries with machine-readable records were merged to investigate the feasibility of using their databases for the development of a union catalog. A comparison of this merged sample with those of the other libraries found that overlap ranged from 21.538 to 71.429 percent. The report concluded the high rate of overlap demonstrated that benefits could be gained from a union catalog. The author noted that the "sample survey shows conclusively that there is a high duplication rate and an even larger 'similarity' rate, i.e. there is a strong chance that the books of a particular author will be found distributed over the V.I.C. network; the key titles will be in several collections, but the older or less popular works will be scattered, so that individually each college will only have an incomplete selection, but together, the colleges may be able to produce a comprehensive collection." Among the eighteen recommendations for cooperation were suggestions for a union catalog of monographs, a union list of serials, development of computer-based cataloging files for cooperative cataloging, interlibrary loan and courier service for document delivery, and subject specialization for collaborative collection development.[34]

Two studies in the mid-1970s explored the possibility of library cooperation among California academic libraries: one focused on periodicals and the second on monographs. The periodicals study by Donald D. Thompson and Richard M. Dougherty examined the possibility of cooperation to share a regional storage facility among three northern University of California System campuses (Berkeley, Davis, and Santa Cruz), two California State University and College campuses (San Jose and San Francisco), and a private university (Stanford). The investigation analyzed data for total periodicals holdings, unique holdings, overlap, volumes held for each title, number of shelf feet occupied by periodicals, circulation of volumes and sets, and characteristics of the periodicals, for example, publisher, language, character-set, frequency. The investigators found 146,000 separate sets of periodicals owned by the six campuses; these represented 90,000 different periodicals of which 56,800 titles were uniquely held. Individual collection sizes ranged from 69,300 titles at Berkeley to 4,420 titles at San Francisco. Stanford held 25,800 titles, but the researchers noted that several of its important and unique collections were not included in the study and urged care in interpreting data which included the Stanford holdings. The number of unique holdings decreased with size of periodical collections: Berkeley, 37,900 titles or 54.7 percent unique; Stanford, 11,700 titles or 34.4 percent unique; Davis, 5,460 titles or 25.5 percent unique; Santa Cruz, 1,240 titles or 11.8 percent unique; San Jose, 500 titles or 8.2 percent unique; and San Francisco, 210 titles or 4.6 percent unique. Excluding Stanford's data from the calculations increased the number of unique titles held by each of the five public institutions with Berkeley then holding 52,600 or 79 percent unique titles. The degree of overlap between ordered pairs ranged from 86.9 percent (Berkeley and San Francisco) to 4.8 percent (San Jose and San Francisco). The correlation of circulation records with holdings resulted in an important finding related to duplication: titles held by only one campus exhibited demand rates which were appreciably lower than demand for titles owned by two or more campuses. These data suggested that titles had not been unnecessarily duplicated and that duplicated titles tended to be in high demand. The researchers stated that this finding provided justification for multiple copies. The findings drawn from the analysis of characteristics of the periodicals holdings and circulation data, while not relevant to this review, make this a valuable resource for collection management.[35]

In the second California study, William Cooper, Donald Thompson, and Kenneth Weeks examined duplication as a factor in planning for cooperative programs such as acquisitions, cataloging, and interlibrary loan. A random sample of 1,024 monograph titles selected from the University of California at Berkeley was checked for duplication in a "northern cluster" of academic libraries. A second sample of 1,003 monograph titles drawn from the University of California at Los Angeles (UCLA) was checked for duplication in a "southern cluster" of academic libraries. The rate of duplication for the Berkeley sample checked in the three northern campus libraries ranged from 4.8 percent (San Francisco) to 25.6 percent (Davis). The average rate of duplication for sample titles held by one of the other northern campus libraries was 30.9 percent. For the UCLA sample, the rate of duplication among the four southern campus libraries ranged from 25.8 percent (Irvine) to 36.2 percent (Santa Barbara) with an average rate of duplication of 49.8 percent. The researchers also compared duplication of each sample with the collection of the other sample library. The Berkeley sample was duplicated 50.1 percent of the time at UCLA. The UCLA sample was duplicated 58.4 percent of the time at Berkeley. These statistics were for approximate matches which included titles with variant imprint, editions, and so forth; the rate dropped slightly when only exact matches were counted. The researchers stated that they were presenting data from the study but not preparing conclusions on its implications for library cooperation.[36]

The eight institutions that form the Boston Theological Institute examined the rate of duplication for their 1973 imprint titles processed through March 1, 1975 which were classified in the BL to BX range. There were 4,789 copies of the 2,336 titles examined or 2.05 copies for each title in the sample. Of these, 1,261 titles or 54 percent were uniquely held. Data were not arrayed to present duplication among ordered pairs of libraries, but the number of unique titles held by individual members ranged from 72 titles (3% of the total sample) to 367 titles (15.7%). The researchers developed a quotient which rated degree of uniqueness to help synthesize the statistical data into meaningful information.[37]

In 1975, Douglas Down and Wesley Young undertook a far-ranging study on the feasibility of catalog card services for all schools in Australia. Among the many issues examined, they studied the level of duplication among the card services offered by each state and the degree of overlap of titles purchased for the schools. The extent of services offered by each state varied from full cataloging on demand for all schools to cataloging of select titles available on request to a limited number of schools. From the six state services the researchers merged 2,505 main entry cards falling within pre-selected alphabetical sequences. Of these, 1,750 or 70 percent of the titles were uniquely cataloged. The percentage of unique titles cataloged by each card service ranged from 69 percent for Western Australia (full cataloging on demand for all schools) to 11 percent for the Victoria primary school service (cataloging for selected titles upon request). When the data were arrayed by ordered pairs, overlap ranged from a high of 65.625 percent of Queensland's records (which provided cataloging data by means of cataloging bulletins) duplicated by Western Australia and a low of 3.16 Western Australia's records duplicated by Queensland. While not reported by the researchers but readily apparent from the tables in the study, the highest degree of overlap was in a comparison of any of the services with Western Australia which cataloged a substantially higher number of titles than any other state service. To examine the degree of overlap for titles purchased by the schools, main entry cards were requested from 200 schools with an enrollment of 200 or more students. Only 78 schools were able to provide the data, returning 4,105 main entry cards. Of these cards, 1,568 titles represented 1,642 unique editions appearing in 2,125 unique impressions. Down and Young reported 43.36 percent of the titles were unique and 77.34 percent were replicated. A second analysis calculated on impressions indicated that 37.17 percent of the impressions were unique with 67.48 percent replicated. The authors concluded that replication would likely be higher with the inclusion of schools enrolling fewer than 200 students. Further, they noted that given the availability of a finite number of acquirable editions, an increase in total bookstock would likely increase the rate of duplication for any particular edition.[38]

Also in 1975, Blair Stewart reported on an ambitious effort by ten liberal arts colleges to share periodical holdings. The Periodical Bank of the Associated Colleges of the Midwest subscribed to needed but low demand titles and filled interlibrary loan requests from the shared titles. As part of the description of the Bank, Stewart reported that one unexpected discovery was the large number of periodicals held by only one library, 2,347 titles or 57.2 percent of the total 4,106 titles held by the group. An additional analysis revealed that only 1,242 or 30.2 of these were current subscriptions. The remainder were periodicals which had ceased publication (350 or 8.5%) or titles which had been canceled recently (755 or 18.3%). Stewart found a high level of diversity among the colleges' subscriptions, with only 73 of the titles among the current subscriptions of all ten libraries. Use of periodicals was discussed and Stewart noted "The data...tend to suggest that the number of libraries subscribing to a title is an indication of its probable usefulness for a liberal arts college" and recommended further investigation of his discovery that demand per title increased directly with the number of libraries holding the periodical. Stewart commented on the lack of use of many titles (measured as requests between libraries) and suggested that libraries spend thousands of dollars on periodicals of doubtful utility.[39]

The availability of machine-readable bibliographic records offered researchers in New York an opportunity to examine collection overlap specifically in the context of cooperative collection development. Using OCLC tapes for four academic libraries, G.T. Evans, R. Gifford, and D.R. Franz analyzed records cataloged in a twelve-week period. They found that 86.7 percent of the titles were unique to one library only. However, they also cautioned that the results were severely limited by the brief period of cataloging time from which the sample was drawn.[40]

David Kaser and Jinnie Y. Davis examined collection overlap as one aspect of their investigation of the viability of merging the libraries of three liberal arts colleges. The rates of duplication ranged from 52 to 66 percent for a shelflist sample of total holdings and from 55 percent to 63 percent for recent acquisitions (1968-1977 imprints). They also examined triplication, the level at which a title was held by all three libraries, and found that only 10 percent of the recent acquisitions were held by all three libraries. They suggested that the rates of duplication were not surprisingly high given the similarities in academic programs offered by the three schools. They calculated a potential savings of \$3,600 per year through coordinated acquisitions but suggested that this would be offset by the costs required to sustain any process established to reduce duplication.[41]

Elizabeth Ward Smith also used machine-readable records from the OCLC database to experiment with developing a methodology for collection development and to establish quantitative guidelines for selection. An initial sample of 22,470 records, every fiftieth title in the OCLC database as of April 1, 1975, was extracted. To make the study manageable, Smith used a smaller sample of 1,481 titles classified in the pure sciences. She analyzed these records for overlap among 34 academic institutions which offered doctoral degrees and promoted advanced research in the subject. Two other "control" college libraries were used for comparison. The 36 libraries held 685, or 46 percent, of the titles in the pure sciences. Individual holdings ranged from 210 titles to 9 titles with one library owning none of the titles in the sample. The largest number of holdings were in libraries located in Ohio, leading Smith to conclude that the database reflected the length of time that these libraries had been cataloging on OCLC. The 685 titles held by the study libraries were represented by 2,144 copies for a rate of duplication of 3.13 copies per title. There were 347 titles or 50.6 percent uniquely held. Additional analyses examined selection procedures and relationship of the materials to the curricula of the institutions. Smith surveyed the selection practices of the libraries and in her recommendations noted that the OCLC database could be viewed as a selection tool because holdings added to the database had been selected by subject experts, either librarians or teaching faculty, or both.[42]

In the first study using data only for public libraries, Charles H. Davis and Debora Shaw investigated overlap among U.S. and Canadian public libraries. They found a range of duplication from 14 to 62 percent and presented additional evidence that overlap is a function of size. A sample of 100 monographs published no earlier than 1970 was selected from each of three American libraries in Indiana and two Canadian libraries in Alberta. Each sample was checked in five public libraries of different sizes, measured by number of volumes, in the other country. The findings indicated that within the range of public library sizes examined for the study the relationship seemed linear; however, the authors made no claim for linearity at extremely high collection sizes. The researchers also checked the sample at academic libraries and suggested that the percentage of overlap would drop substantially in a comparison between types of libraries. This confirms Arms' finding that collection diversity depends more on type of library than on size. For this analysis, the researchers accepted "approximate matches" and treated British and American editions as the same work.[43] A subsequent analysis distinguished between British and American editions, paperback and hardback editions, and other factors that define a bibliographic entity. The overlap rate was not substantially reduced, and differences were within the bounds of experimental error and the confidence levels of the study.[44]

In the late 1950s and 1960s, overlap studies were used to investigate the feasibility of *establishing* centralized or cooperative technical processing. In 1979, Debora Shaw and Edward Stockey used an overlap study to *evaluate* participation in networking by small public libraries contributing their records through a processing center. A random sample of 100 records cataloged for all types of libraries through the INCOSLA Processing Center was checked against the holdings of five public libraries. While at least one copy of the sample titles had been cataloged by the processing center, 18 percent were not found in the study's public libraries. At least one of the five public libraries held 20 percent of the titles; the remaining titles were held by two or more of the five libraries. The researchers concluded that libraries of all sizes are important contributors to resource sharing initiatives because they provide access to uncommonly acquired materials.[45]

Few studies have concentrated on overlap among special libraries. In the first research into overlap for this type of library, Susan Dingle-Cliff and Charles H. Davis investigated the duplication of monographs in eight Canadian addiction libraries ranging in size from 500 to 10,500 volumes. The seventy-one titles in the sample were published in 1970 or later and were selected from the Alberta Alcoholism and Drug Abuse Library. Of these titles, 55 were found in one or more of the other addiction libraries. The level of duplication ranged from 20 to 63 percent. The researchers concluded that even the smallest library contributed to an interlibrary loan network. The issue of linear relationship was again addressed with the researchers reporting the data supported a linear relationship between number of volumes held and duplication rate.[46]

In 1979, Herbert Goldhor reported the results of a 1977 study undertaken to examine the nature and extent of public library holdings of adult nonfiction books in the humanities. The study was not designed to analyze data for overlap between pairs of the participating 19 public libraries; however, Goldhor found 18,927 copies for the 6,412 titles in the sample (including multiple copies within a library's collection) for an average duplication rate of four copies per title. The highest rate of duplication was found in the largest public libraries; those serving populations of 500,000 or more duplicated at the rate of 6.7 copies per title. Smaller libraries had lower rates of duplication: 1.1 for libraries serving populations up to 25,000; 1.3 for populations of 25,000 to 99,999; and 1.5 for populations of 100,000 to 499,999. The average for all four groups was 2.6 copies per title. There was a small, but not statistically significant, difference in duplication of titles found in evaluative tools in the humanities (2.7 copies per title) and titles not found in selection tools (2.5 copies per title). Analysis for age of publication found that 70 percent of the titles had been published in the last twenty years. Three-fourths of the titles were classified in literature or history.[47] In a subsequent analysis of the data, Goldhor concluded that "It appears that there is a tendency for the number of copies to increase as titles are found in more [evaluative] tools...the distribution shown differs significantly from what chance alone would occasion, but the strength of the relationship is minimal."[48] Although overlap was not the primary purpose of this study, it is useful for its concern with the possible reasons for duplication.

In her study of overlap and duplication among public and school libraries, Carol A. Doll confirmed the positive correlation and linear relationship between collection size and overlap for these libraries. The study included the public library and two elementary school libraries in each of four communities. A sample of 200 titles taken from one library in each community was checked against the holdings of two other libraries in the same community. Overlap ranged from 5 to 71 percent in all the comparisons. Overlap between the public libraries and the school libraries averaged 50 percent but only averaged 30 percent between the school libraries. Similar results were found for internal duplication (multiple copies of the same title) and nonbook materials. Unlike studies that have found more diversity between types of libraries, Doll found significantly more overlap if the pair included a school and public library rather than two school libraries. She surmised that these findings contradicted the assumption that overlap would decrease if different types of libraries were compared. However, she noted that the overlap rates may have been influenced more by size because the public library collections were larger than the school library collections. Doll also confirmed the linear correlation between collection size and duplication for magazines, science filmstrips, and fiction sound recordings. From these data, Doll concluded that the public and school library collections make unique contributions to the community and are not similar enough to justify eliminating either.[49]

An entirely different methodology for analysis of overlap was explored by William E. McGrath for a large scale study using a random group of fifty academic libraries from the OCLC membership and a sample of 57,000 records extracted from the OCLC database. He stated that the convention of reporting data as ordered pairs of libraries was not effective for large numbers of libraries or titles. He used multidimensional scaling to graph mathematical similarities on a two-dimensional scale. The holdings data for each type of academic library (medical, legal, theological, large university, college, and junior college) formed easily identifiable clusters demonstrating homogeneity of collections for each type. McGrath concluded that the patterns suggested possibilities for cooperative collection development and made observations for each type of library as well as identified areas where further research would be needed in the application of the methodology.[50]

The American Theological Library Association (ALTA) studied duplication of monographs as part of a larger study of possibilities for cooperative storage and the preservation of materials for its members. The need to design a comprehensive preservation program for acidic and brittle books published in the period from 1800 to 1929 resulted in this analysis used to estimate the size of collections of theological monographs published in the time period, 1860-1929, titles which were deemed most critical in terms of preservation. Eighty-two of the 151 member libraries submitted data. A sample of main entry cards from each was used to estimate the total number of titles held collectively and the number in each collection. From this sample, the researchers estimated that the libraries held 998,300 titles published from 1860 to 1929, with collection size ranging from 358 at Western Theological Seminary to 56,877 at Union Theological Seminary. The 998,300 titles were arranged into a single alphabetical list and stratified sampling used to extract a working sample of 1,039 titles, although 14 titles were later found to be outside the sample time period. The analysis of the final sample found that 77.6 percent were published in the United States and the United Kingdom. Not surprisingly, 77.9 percent of the sample titles were in English. The study found that with each successive decade, the number of titles increased. An average of 1.187 volumes were held for each title. One library held 109 titles and one title was held by 68 libraries. Calculating unique titles using the valid sample of 1,026 titles, the study concluded that 21.8 percent were unique. The study did not calculate the rate of uniqueness for individual libraries. In findings consistent with other overlap studies, the researchers concluded that larger collections own the highest proportion of unique titles and that smallest libraries tend to own the smallest. However, for some small libraries, there seemed to be a disproportion between size and total titles held. The researchers concluded that while all ALTA libraries were likely to own some unique titles, a sizeable portion of the endangered books could be found in a relatively small number of libraries. An analysis of scattering determined that 100 percent of the titles were held by 39 of the 82 libraries. One library's holdings accounted for 60 percent of the titles, two for 70 percent, and three for almost 80 percent. An additional check of the 1,039 titles in the sample found that 139 titles or 13 percent had been microfilmed. The report includes 15 tables reporting data, several of which were beyond the scope of this review but present interesting data useful to determine the extent of a preservation need and to assist in planning a preservation program.[51]

Evans' study using OCLC-derived records of New York academic libraries served as a model for a study of overlap in the University of Wisconsin system. Barbara Moore, Tamara J. Miller, and Don L. Tolliver examined the records cataloged by eleven libraries in the Wisconsin system that were using OCLC for current cataloging during the period July 1977 to June 1979. Only 18.16 percent of the titles had two or more location codes, and 1.05 percent had six or more locations. The analysis indicated that overlap was much lower than previously assumed; this low overlap confirmed the findings of the Evans' study. In contrast to Knightly's findings, overlap among the smaller, non-doctoral group of institutions was higher than the overlap between the larger university libraries. The authors suggested that this difference might result from similarity in basic courses offered at the non-doctoral institutions as well as diversity of programs offered at the doctoral institutions. The authors concluded that the libraries seemed to be collecting unique materials and noted that a cooperative acquisitions program built on existing subject strengths should result in larger collections of unique materials. Finally, the authors cautioned that since the study examined only currently cataloged titles, the findings could not necessarily serve as an indication of total collection overlap.[52]

William McGrath and Thomas Hickey again used multidimensional scaling with a sample 58,375 titles in the OCLC database held in four sets of libraries: 15 public and 15 academic libraries randomly selected from the AMIGOS and NELINET members, 50 randomly selected academic libraries, 50 randomly selected public libraries, and 100 randomly selected libraries regardless of type or location. The data were plotted on a graph and displayed strong homogeneous clusters; for example, university libraries formed a cluster as did public libraries. The authors stated that university libraries, which appeared to have more similarity as a group, should diversify more and specifically recommended that large libraries make a much closer analysis of their audiences in order to achieve exhaustive collection development within a variety of specific subject areas. Finally, McGrath and Hickey noted that the statistical analysis demonstrated similarities (i.e., overlap), but the exact characteristics that determined similarity such as size of collection, maturity (age) of collection, or type of library needed further exploration.[53]

Debora Shaw analyzed collection overlap among 40 academic and public libraries in Indiana. She drew two samples: one limited to monographs published before 1980 and selected from the shelf lists of the libraries, and a second sample extracted from OCLC tapes for the most recent six months (June to December 1981) of cataloging activity. In the sample checked against 26 of the 40 libraries, Shaw found that 598 of 3,056 titles or 19.5 percent were held by only one library. She analyzed overlap from several perspectives including overlap among libraries of the same and different types, influence of library size, and influence of publication date and subject of the sample titles. She found that 27.1 percent of the academic titles searched in academic libraries and 41.2 percent of the public library titles searched in public libraries were uniquely held. From her numerous analyses, she confirmed that diversity is greater among libraries of different types, larger libraries hold more unique titles, more recently-published titles are more likely to be duplicated, and level of overlap varies by subject.[54]

Ian R.M. Mowat reported on the level of duplication for pre-1950 library materials held by Edinburgh University and Glasgow University in Scotland. The data, collected as part of an initiative for retrospective conversion of the library catalogs, assisted planning to determine the feasibility of shared cataloging, the potential for further cooperation, and the libraries' contributions to a national database. A sample of 1,713 titles in eight categories was selected from the Edinburgh catalog and checked for holdings at Glasgow. Factors considered in evaluating the data were that both libraries were entitled to the privilege of legal deposit between 1709 and 1836 and that for most of their history both served universities with curricula derived from a common Scottish educational tradition. While these factors could influence the number of materials held in common, the average rate of overlap was 31 percent. Overlap by category varied considerably with the highest, 50 percent, occurring in books published in the United Kingdom between 1800 and 1836, a level probably affected by the depository status of both libraries during that time. The overlap for all categories of books published in the United Kingdom (published before 1800, 33%; published 1837-1899, 36%; and published 1900-1950, 37%) was higher than overlap in any category of foreign books (published before 1800, 14%; published 1800-1836, 20%; published 1837-1899, 26%; and published 1900-1950, 26%). For foreign titles, overlap was higher among more current titles. Mowat suggested that the low rate of overlap demonstrated that the Scottish university libraries contribute significantly to the national database with respect to older United Kingdom publications. Further, he surmised that this contribution would be even greater for foreign titles given the low level of duplication of these titles and the large number of holdings in the two libraries.[55]

Harry Elvin Broadbent researched overlap in the libraries of eight academic institutions offering similar liberal arts programs. In a sample of 519 titles, overlap ranged from 15 to 60 percent with a mean of 26 percent duplication. He concluded that with the exception of one example of a 60 percent overlap, the percentages seemed too low to reduce duplication through coordinated collection development. Broadbent found that holdings of unique titles ranged from 2 to 16 percent with a mean of 5 percent of the sampled titles. He concluded that the findings provided little support for the belief that each library would make a significant contribution to uniqueness in cooperative arrangements. He also found that 20 percent of unique titles held by the sampled libraries were unique for their regional network. In general, he reaffirmed previous research findings: for a homogeneous group of libraries the proportion of unique titles added to a union list would be small, collection diversity seems to depend more on a mix of types of libraries than on size, and similar libraries may have low rates of diversity (uniqueness). This study also sought to determine if there was a correlation between duplication and circulation. Broadbent found no evidence to support his hypothesis that duplicated titles would also be highly circulated.[56]

A study of cataloging practices and monographic collection overlap among seven academic libraries contributing holdings to the Outlier Union Catalogue and the Library Board of Western Australia examined likely gains to be achieved from sharing data among Western Australia libraries. A sample was drawn from three catalogs: 400 monograph titles from the Outlier Union Catalogue and 200 monograph titles each from the Fiction and Nonfiction catalogs of the Library Board. In addition to general overlap, the study analyzed holdings by age category and by classification using the ten main classes in the Dewey Decimal classification scheme. Among the four age categories (no date, pre-1968, 1968-1972, and 1973 or later) the greatest degree of uniqueness for the majority of the libraries was in the category of pre-1968 titles while the 1973+ date category appeared to be the least unique. Percentages of unique holdings for the total sample ranged from 14.4 percent for holdings of one of the academic libraries to 83.5 percent for fiction and 60.7 percent for nonfiction held by the Library Board. The highest percent of unique holdings among the academic libraries was 54.4 percent. The analysis of holdings of academic libraries reported to the Outlier Union Catalogue found that 57.5 percent of the titles were unique and 42.5 percent were duplicated. In comparing overlap between pairs of libraries, percentages ranged from 2.5 to 84.6 percent with larger libraries most often the duplicating partners in paired comparisons. The study reaffirmed earlier findings of greater diversity between different types of libraries. Generally, the level of uniqueness diminished for the more current materials. Overall, the study found that duplication percentages between libraries varied considerably and did not necessarily reflect variations by size of library. Analysis by subjects, age, and size provided clues to reasons for overlap. The study concluded that all factors, for example, subjects, age, and size, contributed to the level of duplication, with size of collection possibly the least important contributor. The major premise of the study, the potential benefits of sharing cataloging data, was supported. The researchers concluded that the level of duplication among the eight libraries was sufficient to result in a reduction of original cataloging through shared bibliographic data.[57]

William Potter examined the machine-readable records for twenty-one institutions participating in the Illinois Library Computer System Network. He found that 69.46 percent of the different titles examined were held by just one library and noted that the duplication rate of 30.54 percent was consistent with other studies. In the array of ordered pairs, the duplication percentages ranged from a low of .5 to 69.2 percent. Potter found that older materials and non-English titles were more likely to be uniquely held. He also confirmed a linear relationship between size of collections and rate of duplication but noted that this relationship has limits. The results suggested that while overlap does increase with size, very large libraries do not duplicate smaller collections as much as might be expected.[58]

In only the second study of special libraries, Sue Stroyan examined overlap between two hospital health sciences libraries. This study analyzed overlap of serial holdings as well as serial titles. A sample from each library was checked against the collection of the other library. The rate of overlap for monographs for the Library A sample was 19.7 percent: For the Library B sample it was 26.3 percent. Data were analyzed for duplication by publication date using four ranges: 1960-69, 1970-75, 1976-80, and 1981-84. Unlike other studies, Stroyan did not find the highest degree of duplication among recently-published titles but found the highest rate of duplication among titles published in 1976-80. For Library A this rate was 53.3 percent, for Library B it was 60 percent. The degree of overlap for serials holdings and titles was similar to the rate for monographs, but serials holdings were influenced by space constraints and retention policies. Stroyan concluded that overlap among hospital health science libraries followed the patterns demonstrated in other overlap studies; that is, extent of duplication for both monographs and serials is influenced by age, size, and type of library. However, this study did not confirm publication date as a predictor of duplication.[59]

In 1985, Thomas Nisonger reported an overlap study using the machine-readable records for seventeen Texas libraries belonging to the Association for Higher Education of North Texas (AHE). The AHE librarians edited the Research Libraries Group (RLG) Conspectus categories to use for their research because they felt that the RLG Conspectus methodology was emerging as a nationally-recognized collection management tool. The study analyzed monographs with a 1982 imprint date which had been cataloged in 1982 or 1983. A summary report stated that 51.9 percent of the titles were unique, while less than one percent were held by ten or more institutions.[60] A subsequent reference to this project indicated that the AHE project found the highest rate of duplication, almost 60 percent, in the social sciences and humanities. In the sciences and fine arts, duplication was 45 percent.[61]

Texas was also the location of a project analyzing the overlap of nursing materials held by academic health center libraries. The researchers used the records in TALON, a union catalog of monographs database, for 1982-1983 imprints and records in NLM Catline, maintained and updated by Marcive, Inc., for records dating from 1977. Titles intended specifically for nursing represented approximately 6 percent of the total records in the two databases: 1,649 records in TALON and 2,683 records in NLM Catline. Duplication between pairs of libraries ranged from a low of 21.1

percent to a high of 50 percent. Further analysis of the eight libraries serving nursing schools found that duplication of titles with imprint dates 1977-80 ranged from 37.1 to 72.4 percent, titles with imprint dates 1977-83 ranged from 40.2 to 74.3 percent, and titles with imprint dates of 1982-83 ranged from 26.8 to 65.7 percent. The researchers concluded that "An important result of this study, then, is...the confirmation of the similarities of collections."[62]

Sue Stroyan expanded her earlier work investigating overlap among health sciences libraries for her dissertation. She drew a proportionate sample of 775 monograph titles from eight health sciences libraries in a midwestern resource sharing consortium. Holdings of the titles from each library were checked in the other libraries' collections. The data were analyzed for overlap of exact and approximate matches, overlap by subject, and overlap of titles included in the Brandon/ Hill list.[63] She found that 438 exact matches or 56.5 percent were held uniquely. For approximate matches, 379 titles or 48.9 percent were held uniquely. Stroyan also compared the complete serials holdings for overlap of titles and length of holdings, overlap by subject, and overlap of titles in the Brandon/ Hill list. The eight libraries held 671 serial titles with 364 or 54.2 percent held uniquely. From her analyses of length of holdings she found that uniquely held serial holdings ranged from 7 to 68 percent and were related to size of library. Stroyan concluded that two factors identified in previous studies, library size and subject, predict overlap. She found that both monograph and serials titles on the Brandon/ Hill list were more likely to be duplicated thus demonstrating a positive correlation between the listing in a standard bibliography and duplication. Further, the diversity and strengths found for smaller libraries in previous studies were confirmed in her analysis of collections in health sciences libraries.[64]

The feasibility of a national centralized processing center for school media centers in South Africa was investigated by Sandra Olën. She drew a sample of 1,684 nonfiction monograph titles selected for secondary schools by the Transvaal Education Media Services, the most sophisticated of the nine school library services in South Africa. This sample was searched in the South African Bibliographical and Information Network (SABINET) which was created in 1984 and included UKMARC, LCMARC, WLN, and some locally contributed bibliographic records. She found 78.6 percent of the sample titles in SABINET: 1,125 exact matches representing 66.8 percent and 198 approximate matches representing 11.8 percent of the sample. Of the 361 records not found, 146 were for local publications. Olen also compared the titles selected for 1981 by the Cape Education Library Service and compared these to titles selected by the Transvaal service. These 775 titles comprising reference, nonfiction, and fiction records suitable for secondary schools were searched in the Transvaal lists for 1977 through 1983. She found that 288 exact matches (38.1%) and 12 approximate matches (1.6%) for a total of 300 records or 39.7 percent of the books selected by the Cape Education Library Service had been selected by the Transvaal service. In a third test of overlap, Olën extracted a sample from the titles supplied to media centers in secondary schools by the Transvaal Education Media Service for the period 1972 to 1984, omitting books about electronics and motor mechanics and books in the French, German, and Bantu languages. The 80 sample titles included 61 English and 19 Afrikaans titles for 1981, 1982, and 1983: All were nonfiction except one reference work, one work of poetry, and one work of fiction. This list was sent to a stratified sample of nineteen Natal provincial secondary schools for white students. The Natal Education Library Service does not prepare selection lists nor provide centralized acquisitions or cataloging services. While Olën did not summarize these findings in her thesis; the data were displayed as a table of holdings for the seventeen returned lists. Data derived from this table indicate that all of the schools held at least one title on the list with one school holding 25 of the titles. Fifty-five or 68.75 percent of the 80 titles were held at least once with one title replicated twelve times. The fifty-five titles were represented by 178 volumes. For her thesis, Olën concluded that a centralized processing center could provide materials economically for the media centers of South Africa.[65] In a subsequent article, Olën revisited the Transvaal-Natal data and noted that larger numbers of replicated books were found in the larger collections, enabling her to conclude that library size is a predictor of overlap. From her analysis of the data and the selection policies practiced by the education media services, she also concluded that it would not be feasible to have centralized selection for all materials for media centers in South Africa. However, she suggested that it would be possible to compile a comprehensive selection list from which media centers could select between 40 and 70 percent of their acquisitions in order to take advantage of bulk purchasing and centralized processing.[66]

The pending merger of the John Crerar Library with the University of Chicago Library initiated a survey to estimate the duplication of volumes and titles between the two collections. A sample from the Crerar library was compared to the holdings in the University of Chicago Library. The data were analyzed by subject groupings and format (books and serials; bound and bindable volumes). The survey concluded that Crerar's collection in September 1980 included about 237,000 bound or bindable volumes which duplicated holdings of the University of Chicago, of these about 77,000 were book volumes and about 160,000 were serial volumes. Unique bound or bindable volumes were estimated at 352,000 volumes, with about 151,000 of these unique book volumes, about 201,000 unique serial volumes, and about 27,000 rare book volumes. The total number of volumes held was estimated at 616,000, indicating a duplication rate of 38.4 percent. The actual merger between the Crerar and Chicago collections found 649,638 physical volumes, about 24,000 fewer duplicate monographs and about 39,000 more duplicate serials volumes, resulting in a total variation of about 15,000 more duplicate volumes. The revised overlap rate was 38.8 percent.[67]

Blanche Browne investigated duplication as a factor that might influence a school system's decision to participate in a bibliographic utility. Using a stratified sample, she selected four high school libraries from twenty-two in the DeKalb County School System. These four represented a variety of demographic and organizational factors but were compared on the basis of large (over 1,400) and small (less than 1,400) student populations for the duplication study. Browne examined all monograph purchase orders for 1982-83, 1983-84, and 1983-84 to identify orders for duplicate and unique titles. During these three years, the four schools ordered 3,369 titles of which 365 or 10.9 percent were duplicated. Browne noted that this rate of duplication was lower than that found by other duplication studies involving school libraries. A higher rate of duplication was found between the two small school libraries, 12.6 percent, than the two larger libraries, 8.76 percent. The highest level of duplication,

16.71 percent, occurred in a comparison pairing a small with a large library. However, Browne did not draw a conclusion about the relationship of size to overlap. All but one of the duplicate titles and all but seventeen of the remaining unique titles were found in the OCLC database. Of the seventeen unique titles not found, seven were not received by the ordering library, perhaps signalling a problem with the bibliographic citation. Browne concluded that participation in a bibliographic utility could not be recommended solely on the factor of duplication. However, she identified other factors, such as centralized cataloging and the availability of machine-readable records to develop a union list that would facilitate use of unique materials for resource sharing, as reasons for joining a bibliographic utility.[68]

Stella Bentley collected data on the overlap of titles among three institutions offering doctoral level programs in psychology to examine the relationships among characteristics of psychology collections in research libraries. A random sample representing approximately five percent of the monographs in the BF classification was drawn from the shelflist of each library and checked in the catalog of the other two libraries. The overlap ranged from 49.7 to 77.9 percent for approximate matches and from 43.9 to 72.2 percent for exact matches. Bentley found that 24.6 percent of the total sample was held by only one library, and 75.6 percent was held by two or more libraries. She noted that these levels for duplication were higher than overlap for general collections but consistent with findings for duplication of social science material at doctoral level institutions. Bentley also confirmed that unique titles were more likely to be older, non-English titles.[69]

The Australian Bibliographic Network (ABN) explored methods for using its bibliographic database to provide management information for resource sharing. Three approaches were used: *overlap* for titles held by more than one library, *unique* for titles held by only one library, and *gap* for titles not held by any libraries. The overlap study used a random sample of entries made to the ABN microfiche catalog. The results of this approach were not presented due to the very small sample size with the author stating that the results were similar to findings for the other approach. The unique study analyzed a sample of 400 machine-readable records extracted from the ABN bibliographic file. Thirty-nine percent had holdings attached while 61 percent were not held by any reporting library. Of the titles held, 51 percent were held uniquely. The researcher attributed the high level of uniqueness to the short period of time in which holdings had been reported to the ABN and the lack of retrospective records in the database. The gap study found 90 percent of the titles listed in a standard bibliography in theoretical psychology were held by participating libraries. The study confirmed the ease with which such analyses could be conducted using the ABN database but did not draw conclusions from the findings because of the small size of the samples.[70]

In 1988, the OCLC and RLG databases were used for collection analysis for members of the Committee on Institutional Cooperation (the Big Ten universities and the University of Chicago). A sample of 500 machine-readable records for materials published between 1978 and 1983 was selected for two subject areas, botany and mathematical analysis. Holdings from the online databases were recorded, and, in some cases, local catalogs were searched to insure complete data. Duplication between matched pairs of libraries ranged from 30.1 to 60.7 percent in botany and from 32.7 to 70.7 percent in mathematical analysis. Approximately 45 percent of the botany titles and 22 percent of the mathematical analysis titles were not held by any of the libraries, and approximately 25 percent of the titles in each sample were held by only one library. The researchers discussed the considerable problems in using machine-readable bibliographic records for collection analysis and concluded that the pattern of cataloging practices require local validation of holdings to achieve reliability. As a result of the finding that only approximately 5 percent of the acquisitions were unique, the researchers suggested that a change in acquisitions patterns could reduce the amount of material not acquired by any of the member institutions.[71]

Boston Library Consortium, a multitype library cooperative of ten college and university libraries, Boston Public Library, and the State Library, analyzed the machine-readable records for 1981-1985 monographs cataloged by its members. The collection analysis project supported cooperative collection development and provided data for analysis of local and consortium collection strengths and weaknesses. The study used the methodology and adapted the conspectus ranges initially developed for a similar project of the Association of Higher Education (Texas).[72] The analysis of the records identified 603,206 items, representing 289,760 distinct titles of which 176,961 were held by only one institution. Fewer than one-half of the titles, 42 percent, were held by two or more member libraries. Equally important, all member libraries contributed some unique titles to the collective resources. The report consists mainly of graphs: 23 graphs depict the distribution of total records and uniquely held titles among the members for each of the 23 subjects included in the analysis; three graphs highlight the distribution patterns for uniquely held and total records in the humanities, social sciences, and the sciences and technology; and three graphs display the cumulative overlap (titles held by 1, 2, 3, etc. libraries) for each of the 23 subject areas. The report generally concludes that, consistent with other overlap studies, a high percentage of titles are held by only one institution and collection diversity increases with size and type of library. The analysis found consistent levels of overlap for each of the subjects with the percentage of unique titles ranging from 37.1 percent in chemistry to 75.6 percent in physical education.[73] A subsequent article reported on an analysis with an additional 344,000 records for 1986-88 imprints to verify and expand the data analyzed in the first analysis.[74] Results of this study are reported later in this chronological review.

Jane Rozek conducted a small-scale study of the duplication of fiction titles among a public library youth services department and three school media centers. She selected twenty-five titles from the *Junior High School Library Catalog*. All of the titles were held by the public library, although five of them were in collections other than the youth services department. When the catalogs of the three school media centers were checked, only three of the titles were held uniquely by the public library. The average rate of duplication was 3.12 copies per title. She concluded that there were many similarities in the collections despite the different missions of the public and school libraries.[75]

Ruth H. Miller and Martha W. Niemeier studied collection overlap to develop a base from which to study possible collaborative efforts for a statewide network. Using a sample from *Books for College*

Libraries, 3rd edition (*BCL3*), they checked the holdings of four
Indiana university libraries. Of the 497 titles in the sample, 105 or 21.1
percent were not held. The remaining 392 titles were held by at least
one of the four libraries with 222 titles or 44.7 percent uniquely held.
Of the 105 titles not held by any of the four study libraries, 79 titles
or 15.9 percent of the total sample, were available in other libraries
that would eventually be part of the state online network. Another
nine titles were available from other libraries in the state, leaving only
17 titles or 3.4 percent of the sample unavailable from within the state.
The researchers also examined dates of publication and found that
the overlap for number of volumes was greater for titles published
in the 1970s but that the percent of overlap was greater for titles
published in the 1960s. The survey also found higher overlap for titles
in the arts and humanities, followed by the social sciences. The highest
rate of overlap by classification was in the P classification (44.7%),
followed by G-L (33.6%), and C-F (30.1%). The highest rate of
duplication by *BCL3* volume was for titles selected from the third
volume (history) with 9.22 percent of the titles held by three or four
libraries. The least duplication was for titles from volume 5 (science
and technology) with only 5.88 percent of the sample held by three
or four libraries. Overall, overlap ranged from 10.4 percent to 34.2
percent, a finding not unlike previous overlap studies.[76]

The increasing proportion of funds spent for journal
subscriptions led A. S. C. Hooper to examine duplication between
the University of Cape Town and the University of Stellenbosch
in South Africa. The average rate of overlap was 57.99 percent,
with peaks of 68.08 percent in medicine and 67.87 in science.
Hooper noted that the journals supported teaching and research,
and suggested that reducing overlap in libraries can best be achieved
by reducing overlap of teaching and research in the parent
institutions. Further, duplication provides accessibility in the same
way as departmental duplication of staff, equipment, and so forth.
As a result of the study, seven recommendations were prepared with
most seeking to strengthen resource sharing through interlibrary
loan, improved document delivery, and joint planning for
cooperation.[77]

In the late 1980s the Amigos Bibliographic Council and OCLC
collaboratively developed a compact disc product for collection

analysis. This computerized Collection Analysis System derived from work done for the Association of Higher Education in Texas.[78] The compact disc product allows a library to compare its holdings to a subset of records from the OCLC database and to develop a profile of its own collection using the conspectus format. A report by librarians at Southern Methodist University and staff at Amigos detailed use of the CD-ROM product to analyze collections in four SMU libraries as a basis for planning future collection development. In addition, information on overlap between collections was needed for decisions on configuring the automated system which would be shared by SMU libraries. Four collections were analyzed with particular emphasis on identifying overlap between pairs of libraries in the subject areas of philosophy and religion, political science and law, and Latin and North American history. Where high overlap was expected, the project found that overlap ranged from 8 percent in Christianity to 14 percent each in History of the Americas and Political Theory. A high level of overlap in Political Theory was not unexpected because all four libraries collected in the subject. Subjects with low overlap ranged from 0 to 3 percent in the sciences and from 2 to 6 percent in the humanities and social sciences. In some areas, low overlap reflected a policy of avoiding unnecessary duplication when more than one library collected heavily in a subject; for example, History of Mexico collected by two libraries overlapped by 11 percent. The analysis of 610,000 unique titles representing 682,000 records in the database found an overall overlap of 10 percent. The authors reported that the Collection Analysis System was useful in documenting efforts to reduce unnecessary duplication and identifying areas where attention to cooperative efforts should be given. They also noted that the shared database would enable the libraries to retain autonomy in collection development but minimize further overlap.[79]

The cancellation of 10 percent of the serials held by the Chemistry Library at the University of Texas led to an assessment of its remaining serials collection. The *Chemical Abstracts Service Source Index* (*CASSI*) was used to compare duplication of chemistry serials titles with the serials collections of the University of California at Berkeley and the Massachusetts Institute of Technology. Chemical Abstracts provided information on holdings of titles reported in

CASSI. Of the total titles owned by both Texas and Berkeley, they held in common 7,063 titles which represented a 30.6 percent rate of duplication. Overlap between Texas and MIT was similar with 30 percent or 4,791 of the titles duplicated. Overlap increased when only currently-published titles were studied. Texas and Berkeley collectively subscribed to 7,228 titles with 2,810 or 38.9 percent held by both. Texas and MIT subscribed to 4,707 titles and duplicated 1,764 or 37.5 percent of these. The researcher did not draw any conclusions about overlap from these data. However, other data related to use of the serials led to the conclusion that the serials collection at Texas needed supplementing. Subject comparisons enabled her to identify strengths and weaknesses in the collection.[80]

Only one study in this review focused exclusively on elementary schools. Patricia Kugel examined duplication to consider implications for resource sharing. Seven elementary schools in DeKalb County, Georgia, which were using an identical circulation system, were selected and studied for duplication of titles classified as 600-699.99 in the Dewey Decimal Classification. The schools ranged in age from 1 to 35 years with student populations that ranged from 430 to 736 students. The size of monograph collections ranged from 6,828 titles to 10,210 titles. Kugel found that 67 percent of the titles were unique. She found that the newest school had the largest student body, largest collection of titles in the 600s, and the largest percentage of unique titles, 87 percent. The titles held by this one school represented 24 percent of the titles in the sample. Excluding this school reduced the level of unique titles to 61 percent. The highest rate of duplication, 51 percent, was in Dewey 600 and the lowest, 27 percent, was in Dewey 690. No title was found in all seven libraries and only one title was found in six collections. Kugel did not present her data as paired comparisons but from her aggregate data determined that the collections were largely unique and suggested that this could provide a foundation for resource sharing. She noted that the circulation systems, while identical, did not support networking capability.[81]

James F. Govan briefly mentioned a cooperative acquisitions agreement among the University of North Carolina at Chapel Hill, Duke University, and North Carolina State University in a presentation made at a 1989 conference on the future of the academic library. He stated that an analysis of the shared database revealed that over the period of online cataloging, the three institutions had only duplicated 6 percent of their acquisitions, with the highest rate of duplication between any two of the institutions reaching 11 percent. The study methodology was not described.[82]

Kathleen Rae Brown analyzed overlap, internal duplication, and circulation in the library collections of three liberal arts colleges in Maine. Using a systematic random sample, each college library shelflist contributed 1,100 titles to the sample of monographs from the circulating collections. She determined that the three collections were strikingly similar in subject and language distribution with English-language materials predominating. Overlap for approximate matches ranged from 34.8 to 50.6 percent, with overlap the highest when either of the two smallest libraries (321,000 and 380,000 volumes) was compared with the largest (624,000 volumes). Rates for overlap using only exact matches were somewhat lower and ranged from 28.1 to 41.4 percent. The rates of overlap were not constant for date of publication with only the largest library demonstrating a higher overlap rate for older materials. In general, Brown confirmed that overlap depends on age and size of the libraries and that the percent of overlap generally increases with the size of the library. Unlike Broadbent, who found that liberal arts colleges have similar collections of recent materials, Brown did not find that overlap for the Maine libraries was markedly higher for any age category. She noted that a formal coordinated collection development program might not be necessary because recent acquisitions were not resulting in more homogeneous collections. However, she added that cooperation might extend coverage, thus increasing the number of titles available to the group. In her analysis for the influence of standard selection tools (*Books for College Libraries*, 2nd ed.; *Opening Day Collection*, 3rd ed.; and three annual lists, "Outstanding Academic Books and Nonprint Materials," from *Choice*), Brown found that titles listed in the aids were duplicated more often. Further, she found that titles which circulated were likely to be duplicated, but concluded that knowing a title was duplicated could not predict that it would circulate.[83.]

The Network of Alabama Academic Libraries (NAAL) examined overlap among its then seventeen academic members offering graduate programs in teacher education. Machine-readable bibliographic records for monographs cataloged through 1986 in the Library of Congress classification L were extracted from OCLC and analyzed using the methodology developed for the Association of Higher Education (Texas). Unlike previous research, the study did not use a sample but concentrated, instead, on an analysis of all monographs in the Library of Congress L classification. Further, because all participants had recently completed retrospective conversion for their education collections, these 184,900 education records represented all but approximately 4,000 volumes published prior to 1976 held by the NAAL members. The study found that 51 percent of the records were unique, that is, held by only one NAAL institution. An additional 15 percent of the materials were held by only two institutions. A high rate of diversity (uniqueness) was found in the collective resources of the NAAL members with duplication in education holdings averaging only 2.6 volumes for each title. The NAAL study confirmed the linear relationship between size, measured by number of volumes held, and rate of duplication. Thus, Merritt's initial finding that, in general, the larger the library the more likely it was to duplicate the holdings of a smaller library was again confirmed. NAAL also found that all libraries, regardless of size, held some unique titles.[84]

In a 1992 article, Ann C. Shaffner, Marianne Burke, and Jutta Reed-Scott described the collection analysis project of the Boston Library Consortium and expanded on their previous report of the data.[85] This article is an essential supplement to their first report because it includes information on project goals, project management and methodology, and records processing. The Consortium analyzed records for current imprints, including monographs, sound recordings, scores, and microforms but excluding serials and a variety of materials not classed in Library of Congress, such as federal and state publications, medical collections, theses, juvenile literature, and non-Roman language publications. The initial 1989 report detailed findings for imprints dated 1981-1985. This article includes data for a subsequent analysis of 344,000 cataloging records with 1986-1988 imprints. In this article, the researchers reported that the most significant finding was that approximately 62 percent of the total titles with imprint dates 1981-1988 were held by only one library. All twelve libraries held some unique titles and contributed significantly to the collective resources of the Consortium. Very few titles were held by all libraries. In general, the number of titles held decreased with each institution added, that is, fewer titles were held in common by six or seven institutions than by three or four. Further, collection diversity increased with differences in collection size and library type. The researchers found distinct holdings patterns in overlap rates with the highest degree of unique holdings in such subjects as agriculture, law, and physical education that reflect specialized collecting by a member library. The lowest rate of unique titles was found in the physical sciences indicating that the collections in these fields are more homogeneous and include a higher percentage of core materials. Four distinct patterns emerged which ranged from a high concentration of items cataloged by one institution to considerable diversification of holdings among all libraries. The dominant pattern was for one institution, typified by collections in art and architecture, law, and performing arts, to catalog between 20 and 35 percent of the total titles and also to hold a larger percentage of uniquely-held titles for the field. The second pattern, for example mathematics, found similar percentages of titles cataloged, but with one institution holding the significant percent of unique titles. In subjects such as music, religion and philosophy, and technology, two or three institutions cataloged about 20 percent each of the total and uniquely-held titles. A final pattern found highly diversified collections, for example in chemistry, economics and business, and political science, with several institutions holding more than 10 percent of the cataloged and uniquely-held titles. To verify the machine processing of the records, uniquely-held titles in mathematics with 1981-1985 imprints were examined more closely. Of these 3,197 titles, popular computer manuals accounted for 52 percent of the unique titles. Juvenile titles represented 3 percent. In both of these areas, the unique titles were concentrated primarily in the collection of the Boston Public Library. Foreign language materials constituted another 7 percent of the unique titles. The remaining 38 percent of the titles appeared to be English-language research-level titles. The overall findings of this study, using nearly one million machine-readable records and one of the largest conspectus-based project undertaken, confirmed the findings of previous overlap studies.[86]

The Southeast Florida Library Information Network (SEFLIN) reported preliminary data for a review of the uniqueness of 3,046,690 titles held by its 15 members that were also OCLC full members. The initial findings revealed that 58 percent of the titles were held by only one member and 80 percent were held by one or two libraries. Only 130 titles were held by the 13 institutions represented by the 15 OCLC libraries. Every library held unique titles with the five largest libraries holding about 80 percent of the unique titles. The study also examined serials titles and found that 61 percent of the serials titles were held by only one member with 82 percent held by one or two libraries. The brief report did not provide any information on the methodology used for the analysis of overlap.[87]

Patricia Dominguez and Luke Swindler briefly mention an overlap comparison of the collections of the three universities participating in the Research Triangle Libraries Network: Duke University, North Carolina State University, and the University of North Carolina at Chapel Hill. After cooperating for six decades on collection development, the Network's shared an online catalog enabled the libraries to analyze overlap among the three collections. A comparison of 2,311,331 OCLC control numbers in the shared catalog found that 76 percent of the titles were uniquely held. Seven percent of the titles were held by all three libraries.[88] Although details of the comparison were not highlighted in the article on cooperative collection development, correspondence with David Carlson, TRLN Executive Director, provided additional information. His chart comparing pairs of institutions reported that unique holdings were 34.4 percent at the University of North Carolina at Chapel Hill, 27.7 percent at Duke University, and 13.6 percent at North Carolina State University.[89]

SUMMARY OF FINDINGS

These studies constitute a substantial body of research into the issues of collection duplication and diversity. From the beginning, researchers struggled with methodological problems for handling large and complex data sets and for controlling bias in the data. Once scientific sampling of the shelf list seemed mastered and bias overcome, the use of machine-readable files offered new challenges. While machine-readable records and computers enhance the ease with which large data sets can be analyzed, problems remain with defining a unique bibliographic entity.

Some findings have remained fairly constant and may approach codification as a set of laws governing overlap studies. Nonetheless, these cannot be accepted as absolute because there are variations among library collections, reasons for duplication, and philosophies of collection development and access. These differences still warrant study when collaborative ventures are considered.

In general, overlap studies conclude that duplication is influenced by size of the collections, age of the materials, and types of libraries compared. The linear relationship between size of collection and rate of duplication is often confirmed. Researchers noted that this relationship has limits; very large libraries do not duplicate smaller collections as much as might be expected. Further, with few exceptions even the smallest libraries hold some unique items. The degree of overlap is also related to level of acquisitions. Libraries that add a higher number of volumes are more likely to hold more titles in common with other libraries. Age of materials also influences duplication. Almost without exception, more-recently published titles are more likely to be duplicated. These studies reported a lower rate of duplication for older materials and reaffirmed the concern first cited from 1906, "Copies of the book thus rapidly become rare and cannot be found years after publication."[90]

The appearance of a title in a standard bibliography influences the degree of duplication. Every study examining the relationship between duplication and listing in a selection tool found a positive correlation between inclusion of the title and duplication. Titles reviewed in standard review sources are also more likely to be duplicated. This finding was consistent for all types of libraries.

Machine-readable records provide more ease with which to analyze duplication by subject. Researchers generally found a higher rate of duplication of monographs among the social sciences and humanities than other subjects. However, these findings are affected by subject specializations of the libraries a study.

The types of libraries compared affects the level of duplication. In the absence of formal cooperative collection development programs designed to reduce duplication, the level of overlap relates to homogeneity of libraries. Size is an important factor for identifying uniqueness but researchers did not agree whether diversity depended more on type of library than on size.

Many of the studies analyzed duplication among academic libraries. For these, degree of overlap was related to academic programs with a tendency for overlap to rise progressively with the level of the academic degree offered. Most of these studies suggested that duplication of library materials was influenced more by duplication of academic programs than other factors.

APPENDIX: SUMMARY OF REPORT FINDINGS OF DUPLICATION RATES

The following table summarizes data reported in the overlap studies reviewed in this paper. For a few studies, the percentages for rate of duplication have been derived from the data given in the reports. The studies are listed in chronological order of publication or presentation date rather than the year of the research, if different from year of publication.

Year Duplication Rate (%)	Low	High	Average	Type of Library(ies)
1906 Fussler (Goldschmidt and Otlet)			40	Research
1942 Bibliographic Planning Committee of Philadelphia			36	Multitype*
1942 Merritt	1.4	56.2		Research
1944 Eaton			59	Research
1948 Blodgett	3	20		Research
1957 Dawson			82.0	University
1958 Besterman				
Cataloging Project			10.3	Research (National)
American Sample			27	
European Sample			37	

(continued)

APPENDIX (Continued)

Year	Duplication Rate (%)	Low	High	Average	Type of Library(ies)
1965	Estes				College
	Monographs	0	90		
	Serials			55	
1965	Stahle			42.8	Research
1968	Nugent			46.9	University
	General Collection	28.1	55.2	39.7	
	Current Imprints	25.1	70.6	46.9	
1968	Parker			48.8	University
	Nonserial Titles	35	77		
	Serial Titles	29.5	56.0	40.5	
1969	Leonard	4	70		University
1970	Bryan				Research
	1968 Acquisitions	29.5	87.7	61.9	
	1969 Acquisitions	13.2	51.7	58.7	
1970	De Vaz and McCall				Research, State, Public
	Serials			6.29	
	Monographs			2.1	
1971	University of Lancaster, National Catalogue Study				Research
	Research Libraries		80.93		
	Special Libraries	.04	50		
	Pre-1920 Imprints				
	Bodleian Holdings	.99	67.89		
	Research Libraries Holdings	29.87	67.89	75.37	
1971	University of Lancaster, Foreign Books Study				Research
	Foreign Imprints, 1950-1967 Imprints				
	English-language Imprints			53	
	non-English-language Imprints			38	
1971	DePew			77.78	Research
1972	Altman				School, Public
	School Libraries	62.8		83.6	
	Public Libraries			52.3	
	Noncore Titles in School Libraries			51.9	

(*continued*)

APPENDIX (Continued)

Year Duplication Rate (%)	Low	High	Average	Type of Library(ies)
1972 Bryan				Research
1969 Acquisitions Rechecked	67.5	91.9	79.7	
1970 Acquisitions (6 libraries)	48.1	86.1	57.4	
1970 Acquisitions (7 libraries)	53.2	92.2	65.1	
1972 McGrath and Simon			34	Multitype*
1972 O'Neill			43.6	Multitype*
1972 Urquhart and Schofield			22.7	Research
1973 Arms	58	99.7	55	Research
1973 Knightly	45.6	64	52.2	University
Recent U.S. Books			52.2	
No Degree Offered	15	58	37	
Bachelor's Degree	34	65	47	
Master's Degree	44	74	56	
Doctoral Level	69	86	76	
1974 Markusen (Rike)	83	72	75	Multitype*
1974 Jacob				School
Total Database			39	
Sociology			34.6	
Science	36	45	41	
1974 Horacek	0	72.3	53.29	University
1974 Thompson and Doughtery	45.3	95.4	36.8	University
1975 Cooper, Thompson and Weeks				University
Berkeley Sample	4.8	25.6	30.9	
Checked at UCLA			50.1	
UCLA Sample	25.8	36.2	49.8	
Checked at Berkeley			58.4	
1975 Lewkowicz, Oliver and Diener			46	University (Theology)
1975 Down and Young				School
Cataloging Records	3.16		65.625	
School Library Holdings			77.34	

(continued)

APPENDIX (Continued)

Year	Duplication Rate (%)	Low	High	Average	Type of Library(ies)
1975	Stewart		42.8		College (Liberal Arts)
1977	Evans, Gifford, and Franz			13.3	University
1977	Kaser and Davis				College (Liberal Arts)
	Total Sample	52	66		
	Recent Acquisitions	55	63		
1978	Smith			49.4	Research
1979	Davis and Shaw	14	62		Public (International)
1979	Shaw and Stockey	17	73	72	Public
1979	Dingle-Cliff and Davis	20	63	55	Special
1980	Doll	.05	71		Public, School
	Between School and Public			50	
	Between Schools Only			30	
1981	Scrimgeour et al.			78.2	Special (Theology)
1982	Moore, Miller, and Tolliver	18.19	31.99		University
1983	Shaw			80.5	University, Public
	Academic Titles in Public Libraries			72.9	
	Public Titles in Academic Libraries			58.8	
1983	Mowat			31	Research
1984	Broadbent	15	60	26	College (Liberal Arts)
1984	Gilbert and Immonen	3.1	84.6		Research
	Academic and Library Board	14.4	83.5		
	Fiction Holdings		16.5		
	Nonfiction Holdings		39.3		
	Academic Libraries Only	45.6		42.5	
1984	Potter	.5	69.2	30.54	University

(continued)

APPENDIX (Continued)

Year	Duplication Rate (%)	Low	High	Average	Type of Library(ies)
1985	Stroyan				Special (Health Sciences)
	Monographs	19.7	26.3		
	Serials	45	57.7		
1985	Nisonger			48.1	University
	Social Sciences, Humanities			60	
	Sciences, Fine Arts			40	
1985	Bowden	21.1	50		Special (Nursing)
	1977-1980 imprints	37.1	72.4		
	1977-1983 imprints	40.2	74.3		
	1982-1983 imprints	26.8	65.7		
1986	Stroyan				Special (Health Sciences)
	Monographs, Approximate Matches			43.5	
	Monographs, Exact Matches			51.1	
	Serials			45.8	
1986	Olen				School
	Cape/Transvaal Exact Matches			38.1	
	Cape/Transvaal Approximate				
	Matches			39.7	
	Transvaal/Natal Comparison			70	
1986	Cairns				Research
	Initial Findings			38.4	
	Revised Findings			38.8	
1986	Browne	5.47	16.71	10.9	High School
1987	Bentley			75.4	Research (Psychology)
	Approximate Matches	49.7	77.9		
	Exact Matches	43.9	72.2		
1987	Rochester			49	Multitype
1988	Sanders, O'Neil, and Weibel				Research
	Botany	30.1	60.7		
	Mathematical Analysis	32.7	70.7		

(continued)

APPENDIX (Continued)

Year	Duplication Rate (%)	Low	High	Average	Type of Library(ies)
1989	Boston Library Consortium			42	Multitype
	Chemistry			62.9	
	Physical Education			24.4	
1990	Rozek			88	Public, School
1990	Miller and Niemeier	10.4	34.2	55.3	University
	P Class			44.7	
	G-L Classes			33.6	
	C-F Classes			30.1	
1990	Hooper		68.08	57.99	University
1990	Kacena et al.			10	University
1990	Johnson	30	38.9		University
1990	Kugel			33	School (Elementary)
1991	Govan			11	University
1991	Brown				College (Liberal Arts)
	Approximate Matches	34.8	50.6		
	Exact Matches	28.1	41.4		
1992	Heath			49	University
1992	Schaffner, Burke, and Reed-Scott			38	Multitype
1993	Curry			42	Multitype
	Serials			39	
1993	Dominguez and Swindler			24	Research

Note: Study includes several types of libraries.

NOTES AND REFERENCES

1.   William Gray Potter, "Studies of Collection Overlap: A Literature Review," *Library Research* 4(Spring 1982): 3-21.

2.   William K. Buckland, Anthony Hindle, and Gregory P. M. Walker, "Methodological Problems in Assessing the Overlap Between Bibliographic Files and Library Holdings," *Information Processing and Management* 11(August 1975): 89-105.

3.   Herman H. Fussler, "Microfilm and Libraries," in *The Acquisition and Cataloging of Books*, papers presented before the Library Institute at the University of Chicago, July 29 to August 9, 1940, ed. William M. Randall (Chicago: The University of Chicago Press, 1940), p. 332. The translated quote is from an article by Robert Goldschmidt and Paul Otlet, *Sur une forme nouvelle du livre: le livre microphotographique* (Bruxelles: Institut International de Bibliographie, 1906), pp. 3-6.

4.   Bibliographical Planning Committee of Philadelphia, *Philadelphia Libraries: A Survey of Facilities, Needs and Opportunities* (Philadelphia: University of Pennsylvania Press, 1942), p. 67.

5.   Leroy C. Merritt, "The Administrative, Fiscal, and Quantitative Aspects of the Regional Union Catalog," in *Union Catalogs in the United States*, ed. Robert B. Downs (Chicago: American Library Association, 1942), pp. 3-128.

6.   Merritt, *Union Catalogs in the United States*, p. 77.

7.   Andrew Jackson Eaton, "Current Political Science Publications in Five Chicago Libraries: A Study of Coverage, Duplication, and Omission" (Ph.D. diss., University of Chicago, 1944).

8.   Catherine C. Blodgett, "Duplication in Original Cataloging Among Research Libraries in the New York Area" (Master's thesis, Columbia University, 1948). Findings from this study were also reported in "Duplication in Original Cataloging Among Six Research Libraries," *College and Research Libraries* 12 (January 1951): 20-23.

9.   John Minto Dawson, "The Acquisitions and Cataloging of Research Libraries: A Study of Possibilities for Centralized Processing," *Library Quarterly* 27(1957): 1-22.

10.   Theodore Besterman, "The European Union Catalogue Project," *Journal of Library Documentation* 14(June 1958): 56-64.

11.   Ruth Estes, *A Study of Seven Academic Libraries in Brooklyn and Their Cooperative Potential* (New York: Council of Higher Educational Institutions in New York City, 1963).

12.   Everett L. Moore, "Processing Center for California Junior Colleges—A Preliminary Study," *Library Resources and Technical Services* 9(Summer 1965): 303-317.

13.   Marilyn Stahle, "The Cooperative Potential of Eight Academic and Research Libraries Based on an Analysis of Current Acquisitions" (M.A. thesis, University of Chicago, 1965).

14.   Willam R. Nugent, "Statistics of Collection Overlap at Libraries of Six New England State Universities," *Library Resources and Technical Services* 12(1968): 31-36.

15.   Ralph Parker, *A Feasibility Study for a Joint Computer for Five Washington, D.C. University Libraries* (Washington, DC: Consortium of Universities of Metropolitan Washington, DC, 1968).

16.   Buckland, et al., "Methodological Problems," p. 98.

17. Lawrence C. Leonard, Joan M. Maier, and Richard M. Dougherty, *Centralized Book Processing: A Feasibility Study Based on Colorado Academic Libraries* (Metuchen, NJ: Scarecrow Press, 1969).

18. Harrison Bryan, "The New South Wales Collecting Project," *Australian Library Journal* 19, 8 (September 1970): 312-317.

19. Harrison Bryan, "A Further Assessment of the New South Wales Area Collecting Scheme," *Australian Library Journal* 21, 8 (October 1972): 375-381.

20. Ursula De Vaz and Lennie McCall, "Duplimania: The State of the Art in W.A.," *Australian Library Journal* 19(September 1970): 309-311.

21. University of Lancaster, Library Research Unit, *National Catalogue Coverage Study: Report to the National Libraries ADP Study* (Lancaster, England: University of Lancaster, 1971).

22. University of Lancaster, Library Research Unit, *Foreign Books Acquisitions Study: Report to the National Libraries ADP Study* (Lancaster, England: University of Lancaster, August, 1971).

23. John N. DePew, "Business and Economic Publications in Four Pittsburgh Libraries: A Study of Coverage, Duplication, and Omission" (Ph.D. diss., University of Pittsburgh, 1971).

24. Ellen Altman, "Implications of Title Diversity and Collection Overlap for Interlibrary Loan Among Secondary Schools," *Library Quarterly* 42(April 1972): 177-194.

25. Bryan, "A Further Assessment."

26. William E. McGrath and Donald J. Simon, "LNR: Numerical Register of Books in Louisiana Libraries" (Baton Rouge: Louisiana State Library, 1972, microfiche). (ERIC Document Reproduction Service Nos. ED 070 470, and 070 471).

27. Edward T. O'Neill, in collaboration with Mary Lynn Seanor, *A Survey of Library Resources in Western New York* (Buffalo, NY: Western New York Library Resources Council, 1972).

28. John A. Urquhart and J. L. Schofield, "Overlap of Acquisitions in the University of London Libraries: A Study and a Methodology," *Journal of Librarianship* 4(January 1972): 32-47.

29. W.Y. Arms, "Duplication in Union Catalogues," *Journal of Documentation* 29(1973): 373-379.

30. John J. Knightly, "Cooperative Collections Development in Academic Libraries: The Relationship of Book Collections to Curricula of Cooperating Institutions" (Ph.D. diss., University of Texas at Austin, 1973). A summary of the research was published in id., "Library Collections and Academic Curricula: Quantitative Relationships," *College and Research Libraries* 39(1975): 295-301.

31. Barbara Evans Markuson, *The Indiana Cooperative Library Services Authority-A Plan for the Future* (Indianapolis: Indiana State Library, 1974). Tables for the search are presented in Appendix A, Section B, "MARC/OCLC Data Base Search," prepared by Galen E. Rike, A81-A86.

32. Markuson, *The Indiana Cooperative*, p. 67.

33.   Gale Sypher Jacob, "The High School Library Collection: An Introductory Study of Six High School Libraries" (Williamsport, PA: Bro-Dart, 1974).

34.   John I. Horacek, *Co-operative Development of Library Services in Affiliated Colleges of the Victoria Institute of Colleges* (Melbourne: Victoria Institute of Colleges, 1974).

35.   Donald D. Thompson and Richard M. Dougherty, "Preliminary Summary Report on the Feasibility of Expanded Library Cooperation Among the Northern Campuses of the University of California: A Study of Periodicals Overlap and Patterns of Use" (University of California, 1974).

36.   William S. Cooper, Donald D. Thompson, and Kenneth R. Weeks, "The Duplication of Monograph Holdings in the University of California Library System," *Library Quarterly* 45(1975): 253-274.

37.   Linda B. Lewkowicz, Peter L. Oliver, and Ronald E. Diener, "Acquisitions Analysis Employing the Statistical Package for the Social Sciences," *Proceedings of the 38th ASIS Annual Meeting* 12(1975): 53-54.

38.   Douglas W. Down and Wesley A. Young. *Cataloguing for Schools: The Feasibility of Catalogue Card Services for All Schools in Australia: A Report to the Australian Schools Commission* (Carlton, Victoria: State College of Victoria at Melbourne, 1975).

39.   Blair Stewart, "Periodicals and the Liberal Arts College," *College and Research Libraries* 36(September 1975): 371-378.

40.   G.T. Evans, R. Gifford, and D.R. Franz, "Collection Development Using OCLC Archival Tapes" (Washington, DC: U.S. Office of Education, Office of Libraries and Learning Resources, 1977, microfiche). (ERIC Document Reproduction Service No. ED 152 299).

41.   David Kaser and Jinnie Y. Davis, *The Viability of Merging Three Academic Libraries in Worcester* (Bloomington: Graduate Library School, University of Indiana, 1977, microfiche), (ERIC Document Reproduction Service No. ED 143 346).

42.   Elizabeth Ward Smith, "Quantitative Guidelines for Building Library Collections in Institutions Offering Doctoral Degrees and Promoting Advanced Research—A Methodology" (Ph. D. diss., State University of New York at Buffalo, 1978).

43.   Charles H. Davis and Debora Shaw, "Collection Overlap as a Function of Size: A Comparison of American and Canadian Public Libraries," *Journal of the American Society for Information Science* 30(1979): 19-24.

44.   Debora Shaw and Charles H. Davis, "Cooperative Cataloging and Automated Bibliographic Networks: Considerations for Public Libraries," *Public Library Quarterly* 4(Winter 1979): 387-397.

45.   Debora Shaw and Edward A. Stockey, "Contributions of Small Libraries to State-Wide Resource Sharing: A Study of Collection Overlap Through the INCOSLA Processing Center," *Public Library Quarterly* 1(Fall 1979): 281-290.

46.   Susan Dingle-Cliff and Charles H. Davis, "Collection Overlap in Canadian Addictions Libraries," *Special Libraries* 70(1979): 76-81.

47. Herbert Goldhor, "A Study of Public Library Book Collections in the Humanities" (Urbana: University of Illinois, 1979, microfiche), (ERIC Document Reproduction Service No. ED 179 189). The results were also summarized in id., "U. S. Public Library Adult Non-Fiction Book Collections in the Humanities," *Collection Management* 3(Spring 1979): 31-43.

48. Id., "Secondary Analysis of Data on a Sample of Adult Titles in the Humanities Held by 20 United States Public Libraries" (Urbana: Library Research Center, University of Illinois, 1981, microfiche), (ERIC Document Reproduction Service No. ED 219 068).

49. Carol A. Doll, "A Study of Overlap and Duplication Among Children's Collections in Public and Elementary School Libraries" (Ph.D. diss. University of Illinois at Urbana-Champaign, 1980). Subsequent articles derived from Doll's dissertation were published as "Overlap Studies of Library Collections in School and Public Libraries," *Public Libraries* 21(Spring 1982): 33-34; "School and Public Library Overlap and Implications for Networking," *School Library Media Quarterly* 11(Spring 1983): 193-199; "A Study of Overlap and Duplication Among Children's Collections in Selected Public and Elementary School Libraries," *Library Quarterly* 54(July 1984): 277-289; and "A Comparision of Children's Collections in Public and Elementary School Libraries," *Collection Management* 7(Spring 1985): 47-59.

50. William E. McGrath, "Implications for Cooperative Collection Development in a Random Group of Academic Libraries: or, Beyond Overlap," in *Options for the 80s*, ed. Michael D. Kathman and Virgil F. Massman (Greenwich, CT: JAI Press, 1981), pp. 287-296.

51. A.D. Scrimgeour, A. Hurd, R.F. Deering, and D.D. Thompson, *Collection Analysis Project: Final Report..* (Philadelphia, PA: Ad Hoc Committee for the Preservation of Theological Library Materials, American Theological Library Association, 1981)

52. Barbara Moore, Tamara J. Miller, and Don L. Tolliver, "Title Overlap: A Study of Duplication in the University of Wisconsin System Libraries," *College and Research Libraries* 43(1982): 14-21.

53. William E. McGrath and Thomas B. Hickey, "Multidimensional Mapping of Libraries Based on Shared Holdings in the OCLC Online Union Catalog"(Dublin, OH: OCLC Online Computer Library Center, July 1983). (OCLC/OPR/RR-83/5)

54. Debora Shaw, "Overlap of Monographs in Public and Academic Libraries in Indiana"(Ph.D. diss., Indiana University, 1983). This research was also discussed in id., "Overlap of Monographs in Public and Academic Libraries in Indiana," *Library and Information Science Research* 7(July-September 1985): 275-298.

55. Ian R.M. Mowat, "Egos: A Study of Stock Overlap in the Libraries of the Universities of Glasgow and Edinburgh," *Catalogue & Index* 69(Summer 1983):1-3.

56. Harry Elvin Broadbent, III, "Collection Overlap and Coordinated Collection Development" (Ph.D. diss., Drexel University, 1984).

57. Annemi Gilbert and Helen Immonen, with the assistance of Susan Davis,

Collection Overlap Implications for Sharing Monograph Cataloguing Among Western Australian Libraries, Western Library Studies 3 (Perth: The Library, Western Australian Institute of Technology, 1984).

58.   William Gray Potter, "Collection Overlap and Diversity in the Illinois LCS (Library Computer System) Network" (Ph.D. diss., University of Illinois at Urbana-Champaign, 1984). The results are also summarized in id., "Collection Overlap in the LCS Network in Illinois," *Library Quarterly* 56(1986): 119-141.

59.   Sue Stroyan, "Collection Overlap in Hospital Health Sciences Libraries: A Case Study," *Bulletin of the Medical Library Association* 73(October, 1985): 358-364.

60.   Thomas E. Nisonger, "Editing the RLG Conspectus to Analyze the OCLC Archival Tapes of Seventeen Texas Libraries," *Library Resources & Technical Services* 29(October/December 1985): 309-327.

61.   Carolyn Kacena, Curt Holleman, Roger Loyd, Ann Armbrister, Douglas A. White, and Catherine C. Wilt. "Collection Analysis and Resource Sharing: The OCLC/AMIGOS Collection Analysis System and the SMU Experience," in *Advances in Library Resource Sharing* 1, ed. Jennifer Cargill and Diane J. Graves, (Westport, CT: Meckler, 1990), p.132.

62.   Virginia M. Bowden, Elizabeth Anne Comeaux, and Sharon Gavin Fought "Comparative Analysis of Monographic Collections in Nursing" (San Antonio: University of Texas Health Science Center at San Antonio School of Nursing, 1985, microfiche). (ERIC Document Reproduction Service No. ED 269 019).

63.   Alfred N. Brandon and Dorothy R. Hill, "Selected List of Books and Journals for the Small Medical Library," *Bulletin of the Medical Library Association* 73(1985): 176-205.

64.   Sue Stroyan, "Collection Overlap of Eight Hospital Libraries in a Health Sciences Consortium" (Ph.D. Diss., University of Illinois at Urbana-Champaign, 1986).

65.   Sandra Irene Isabel Olen, "The Feasibility of a National Centralized Processing Centre for Materials for School Media Centres in South Africa" (Thesis, University of South Africa, 1986).

66.   Id., "Replication in School Media Centres in South Africa," *South African Journal of Library and Information Science* 57(March 1989): 84-88.

67.   Paul M. Cairns, "Crerar/Chicago Library Merger," *Library Resources and Technical Services* 30(April/June 1986): 126-136.

68.   Blanche Gutowski Browne, "Duplication of Monographic Titles in the Acquisitions Process of a School System with Implications for Participation in a Bibliographic Utility" (Ph.D. diss., Georgia State University, 1986).

69.   Stella Bentley, "Inventory, Overlap, and Description of Psychology Collections in Research Libraries: Study of a Conspectus" (Ph.D. diss., Indiana University, 1987).

70.   Maxine K. Rochester, "The ABN Database: Sampling Strategies for Collection Overlap Studies," *Information Technology and Libraries* 6(September 1987): 190-196.

71.   Nancy P. Sanders, Edward T. O'Neill, and Stuart L. Weibel, "Automated Collection Analysis Using the OCLC and RLG Bibliographic Databases," *College*

and Research Libraries 49(July 1988): 305-314.

72. Nisonger, "Editing the RLG Conspectus."

73. Boston Library Consortium, "Collection Analysis Project Report: 1981-1985 Data" (Boston: The Consortium, 1989).

74. Ann C. Schaffner, Marianne Burke, and Jutta Reed-Scott, "Automated Collection Analysis: The Boston Library Consortium Experience," in *Advances in Library Resource Sharing*, 2, ed. Jennifer Cargill and Diane J. Graves (Westport, CT: Meckler, 1992), pp. 35-49.

75. Jane Rozek, "Small-Scale Investigation of the Overlap of School and Public Library Collection Development," *Illinois Libraries* 72(February 1990): 161-163.

76. Ruth H. Miller and Martha W. Niemeier, "A Study of Collection Overlap in the Southwest Indiana Cluster of SULAN," *Indiana Libraries* 9 (1990): 45-54.

77. A.S.C. Hooper, "Overlapping Journal Subscriptions as a Factor in University Library Co-Operation," *South African Journal of Library and Information Science* 58(1990): 25-32.

78. Nisonger, "Editing the RLG Conspectus."

79. Kacena et al. "Collection Analysis and Resource Sharing."

80. Christine Johnson, "Automated Collection Assessment: CASSI as a Tool," *Technical Services Quarterly* 8(1990): 43-54.

81. Patricia Kugel, "Overlap and Unique Titles in Selected Elementary School Media Centers with Implications for Resource Sharing" (Ed. Specialist thesis, Georgia State University, 1990). (ERIC Document Production Servive No. ED 344 608).

82. James F. Govan, "Ascent or Decline? Some Thoughts on the Future of Academic Libraries," in *The Future of the Academic Library*. Proceedings of the Conference Held at the University of Wisconsin in September 1989, ed. Eugene P. Trani, Graduate School of Library and Information Science Occasional Papers, No. 188-189 (Champaign: University of Illinois at Urbana-Champaign, January 1991).

83. Kathleen Rae Brown, "An Analysis of the Variables of Overlap, Duplication, and Use in the Collections of Three Liberal Arts College Libraries" (Ph.D. diss., University of North Carolina at Chapel Hill, 1991).

84. Fred Heath, "An Assessment of Education Holdings in Alabama Academic Libraries: A Collection Analysis Project," in *Cooperative Collection Development, Proceedings of the June 1991 ASCLA Multi-Lincs Preconference*, comp. Diane Macht Solomon, (Chicago: Association of Specialized and Cooperative Library Agencies, 1992), pp. 37-65.

85. Boston Library Consortium, "Collection Analysis."

86. Shaffner et al., "Automated Collection Analysis."

87. Elizabeth Curry, "The Library Without Walls Collection: A Network Collection Analysis," *Exchange, A Newsletter for the Members of Southeast Florida Library Information Network* 4(Spring 1993): 4.

88.   Patricia Buck Dominguez and Luke Swindler, "Cooperative Collection Development at the Research Triangle University Libraries: A Model for the Nation," *College & Research Libraries* 54(November 1993): 470-496.

89.   David Carlson, Personal Communication dated January 12, 1994.

90.   Fussler, "Microfilm and Libraries."

WEEDING ACADEMIC LIBRARIES:
THEORY INTO PRACTICE

Mary Bushing and Elaine Peterson

Academic libraries have a tradition of keeping things. In the past, academic collections were described as research in nature, if not in numbers. One hesitated to withdraw anything at all because it might be needed or useful at some point for some patron. The economic realities of modern librarianship are bringing increasing pressures to bear to hold us responsible for the costs associated with these large and often difficult to use research collections. Further, the nature of academic librarianship itself is changing in response to the shifting reality of the scholarly world.

Several economic and philosophical factors have brought us to a recognition of the need to maintain collections at an optimum size for a particular situation:

Advances in Collection Development and Resource Management,
Volume 1, pages 61-78.
Copyright © 1995 by JAI Press Inc.
All rights of reproduction in any form reserved.
ISBN: 1-55938-213-9

1. The concept of access rather than ownership. This has been enhanced by bibliographic utilities and networks that actually provide us with proof that we are not the only library owning a particular title.

2. Overhead costs for buildings, utilities, personnel, and automated systems. These items have made it increasingly necessary to consider the real costs of maintaining each item.

3. Institutions adopting concepts of down-sizing or at least attempting to maintain enrollments at "optimum" numbers to sustain the existing physical plant and infrastructure.

4. The extent of the "information explosion" is greater than the most futuristic among us could have imagined when discussing it even twenty years ago. We simply had no idea what such a concept would mean in terms of publishing output and the resulting quantity of material.

5. Electronic publishing is demystifying the book and diminishing the reverence which used to make it virtually impossible to discard a book in many institutions. We now recognize that the book is not a permanent item—once produced, destined to exist forever.

6. Collection assessment projects, with the aid of the conspectus, have encouraged librarians in large and small institutions to get into the stacks to examine the quality of the collections in a systematic manner. The results of such collection assessment work is a growing awareness of the difference between quantity and quality, and a realization of our responsibility to be true to our specific institutional mission.

All of these factors have contributed to an awareness of the need, as well as the professional responsibility, to withdraw materials from academic collections.

Despite these and other pressures, Richard M. Dougherty commented in an 1989 editorial that his experience with Association of Research Library (ARL) statistics suggested that the clear possibility existed that academic libraries were not removing "deadwood" from their collections. He pointed out the difficulty of using collections that contained such obvious deadwood as multiple copies, superseded textbooks, or materials no longer in support of an institution's instructional or research program.[1] Does this mean that academic libraries have been ignoring advice to withdraw inappropriate material?

A review of the literature on weeding since the 1950s shows some interesting patterns, but consistent and clear advice on weeding or deselection for academic libraries is not evident. The 1950s and 1960s reveal several articles and dissertations on weeding for academic libraries. Both large universities and small colleges are covered with topics on speed weeding, the costs of weeding, and weeding as an art form. Several articles include guidelines, criteria, and manuals for deselection.

As might be expected, the literature of the 1970s begins to address the problems of library storage and its relationship to collection management and, therefore, weeding. Although there were articles published during the 1970s on weeding, there is a noticeable decline in addressing the topic in the academic sphere. Indeed, through the 1970s and 1980s, the vast majority of articles are on weeding the special library collection (medical, law, sci-tech), the school or media center's collection, or the public library. Academic libraries are mentioned but usually in the context of a small portion of their collection such as maps, music, reference, or rare books.

Just as the 1970s, articles on weeding begin to reflect the issues of library storage, and pieces on serials deselection and book sales abound in the 1980s reflecting the austere fiscal climate and rising inflation. Although great strides were made in the 1980s in advancing modern techniques of collection development such as the Research Libraries Group (RLG) Conspectus, a disproportionate number of articles on weeding are concerned with book sales!

A few articles have begun to appear in the late 1980s and 1990s which raise more interesting issues such as increasing circulation through weeding and automated citation reports as a guide for deselection. However, with the exception of a brief report on team weeding at one university library,[2] library literature of the last decade has lacked much of substance for those weeding an entire academic library collection.

The 1991 publication of the *Guide to Review of Library Collections: Preservation, Storage, and Withdrawal* published as Number 5 of the *Collection Management and Development Guides*

presents a useful review of the literature and an outline of the factors
which contribute to the review process as well as the criteria that
might be established to assist with the process.[3] Criteria and
guidelines for preservation review, storage review, and withdrawal
are each presented in a well organized outline form similar to other
titles in the series. This publication is a welcome addition to the
weeding literature and will prove useful to any library preparing
review criteria for a specific project or for the continuing review that
ought to be part of the collection development process.

If Dougherty is correct in his belief that academic librarians have
failed to get rid of the deadwood in their collections, it is not so much
that we failed to do it because we were wrong or short sighted, but
times and our collective circumstances have changed. We now need
to provide methodologies along with the theory to enable librarians
to engage in weeding activities as part of the general collection
development process. Examples of successful projects and procedures
might assist all of us in designing our own procedures for routine
deselection processes as well as one-time weeding projects. Our
experience at Montana State University, discussed in a latter section
of this paper, revealed more than just a workable model for a weeding
project. It raised issues about library education in preparing
individuals for collection development activities and made us aware
of other factors that need to be addressed if deselection is to become
a routine aspect of academic librarianship.

Almost everyone admits that deselection or weeding is one of the
many procedures that is an essential component for a responsible
collection management program. The theory and practice of such
activity has often been expressed by merely telling present and future
librarians to use the selection criteria adopted for their particular
collection. This advice, however, discourages the thinning of
collections. In using the selection criteria, we are placed in a gathering
or building mode rather than in a frame of mind that encourages
the withdrawal and diminishing of our existing collections. We defeat
our own efforts at thinning the collections by arguing on behalf of
keeping items based on the same criteria we used to place them in
the collection in the first place. Guidelines need to be established for
withdrawal and should be presented in terms that encourage the
process of thinning rather than the processes of growth. Such

guidelines and the individual procedures necessary to implement them require practicality and simplicity. Libraries are very good at preventing particular activities by making the process too complicated. Sabotage can take many forms!

The main reason for weeding, deselecting, or thinning our collections is to check the glut of materials being distributed and collected and to make it possible for our users to identify, find, and use appropriate sources. In order to believe in the need to systematically withdraw materials from our collections, it is necessary to believe that use is in fact inhibited by the large quantity of material, unintentional duplication, inaccurate records, and the evermore daunting task of identifying and judging such resources. We somehow hate to admit any of this. Because we take pleasure in the "hunt" we tend to place a value on the process of finding just the right things. We forget or fail to recognize that the majority of our users, even in an academic library, take little pleasure in the process itself. They want to have the appropriate sources identified and retrieved as efficiently as possible. Thus the departmental secretary or the student assistant is sent to the library to do the initial research or to attempt to retrieve already identified sources. Professors in most of our institutions do not have time to leisurely pursue obscure volumes. There are still those scholars who enjoy the processes of the library, but they are ever more scarce. We continue to maintain collections and processes that cater to the few while frustrating the majority.

Public and school librarians are more likely than academic librarians to actively engage in the task of identifying materials that are no longer appropriate or correct. They believe that they are capable of determining which materials ought to be withdrawn from the collections in order to ease access and provide the best possible product for the users. In a special library, although a sophisticated clientele is often being served, the librarian takes the responsibility to make the collection as efficient as possible by maintaining a collection in keeping with the "just in time" model of modern business rather than the "just in case" model of historical librarianship. In an academic library, we expect our clients to be able to identify and judge the appropriate resources for their purposes and have hesitated to assume that we ought to be the ones withdrawing materials.

Academic librarians often have deferred the responsibility for evaluation and withdrawal of materials by arguing that one can never have too much information or that even the most inaccurate, dilapidated, or poorly written book may contribute to an historical review of the literature. Such reasoning has left many academic libraries filled with materials that stand little chance of ever being used and frustrate the user's attempts to identify and use appropriate items.

At MSU we have implemented procedures for the routine de-selection processes as part of the regular collection development operation. These include the identification of superseded editions or similar items that might need evaluation and possible withdrawal. Technical services staff routinely place previous editions in the review area[4] along with new editions so that the editions can be compared and a recommendation for the possible purchase of the new edition can be made along with a recommendation about the withdrawal, maintenance or preservation of the previous edition(s) at the same time. Sometimes in the process of comparing a new edition to the older one we discover things like new editions that only differ from the previous one by the addition of a five page final chapter. If the new edition costs $60, we are paying at least $12 a page for the new chapter—hardly a bargain by most standards.

We also keep a running list of target subject areas that appear to need closer inspection when time and staff are available. By addressing deselection issues in a routine manner, we attempt to diminish the trauma associated with deselection projects that are perceived as additional work, and that often result in massive withdrawals all at the same time. Such projects are difficult to accept for many academic librarians, while consensus about the fate of an individual title is easier to reach.

Specific deselection projects have been designed to meet the unique needs of our library. One such project involved the review of the entire reference collection by the public services librarians. Recommendations for withdrawal, replacement, transfer to other areas of the collections, and preservation were made by the librarian reviewing a specific subject segment of the reference collection. Titles were grouped in call number sequences and gradually placed in the review area along with each initial recommendation. Colleagues considered these recommendations, consensus was reached or negotiated, and action taken. A similar approach was taken to examine the atlases that are spread across the collection—reference, stacks, branch library, oversized collections. By targeting sections of the collection in this manner and finding a means to address the concerns of librarians, we have managed to create a positive attitude about the concept of evaluation of items within the collections and to place such work in the context of the general collection development process.

At Montana State University, as at many other medium-sized institutions, the library collections have grown to fill the existing building with little hope of a larger facility in the near future. Despite inadequate budgets, new materials continue to put pressure on resources by requiring constant shifting and rearranging of limited shelving to accommodate items. We have not been able to complete retrospective conversion for the entire collection despite automation and bibliographic utilities. Older materials, still in Dewey, have limited access and have very little use. The economics of converting and reclassing these materials made it obvious that at least some effort had to be made to evaluate them before investing further in each one. MSU does not have a large enough library faculty to have specific subject bibliographers. We encourage librarians to be generalists despite their graduate subject strengths. We therefore decided that we had to design a process for review and withdrawal that would enable us to move quickly through these older materials, but provide for adequate review of decisions made by generalists. In the past, items to be withdrawn were placed in the review area to be evaluated by library and instructional faculty, but the size of this project would not allow for such handling of materials.

The first step in any such project is an articulation of the goal, a definition of the scope of the project, an identification of the resources available, an outline of the process, and the establishment of a time line to enable the organization to visualize the project within the reality of day-to-day operations and responsibilities. Because of the circumstances of our situation (seventy years of Dewey-classed collections and almost thirty years of Library of Congress(LC)-classed items with many currently received serial titles in the Dewey stacks to complicate stack management issues), it was decided that the primary goal of the project was to consolidate the Dewey stacks.

To accomplish this we would first of all reclass live serial titles to LC. The second phase was to withdraw unneeded monographs so that the Dewey stacks could be compacted without any growth considerations. At a later date, a thorough evaluation of the closed serials classed in Dewey could be undertaken. Once the reclassing of the current Dewey serials was in progress, it was possible to begin the weeding project for the monographs.

The materials in these sections of the collections were all at least thirty years old. Some were on the Online Public Access Catalog (OPAC) and so did circulate either because of initial machine-readable records or because they had been bar-coded when patrons identified them in the card catalog and brought them to the desk for circulation. Most of our users, however, only use the OPAC and browse only in the LC stacks. Usage, or rather lack of it, therefore could not be a strong reason for withdrawal because of such limited access to the material. Unused items had to be considered with the question: If this were bar-coded and in LC would it get used? The answer was generally still "no" but such questioning helped to make decisions about borderline titles.

The extent of the project was determined by the Collection Development Librarian who estimated the approximate number of monographic shelves by examining the collection itself and counting shelves of books and discounting shelves of serials. This method was actually much easier and faster than trying to estimate from the shelf list. The numbers of monographic shelves were then divided into subject segments of approximately 100 to 120 shelves. Each librarian was assigned a segment, along with general instructions, and a specific month during the following six-months within which to accomplish the weeding assignment. It was essential to assign a month for each librarian's work so that the collection development librarian and the technical services staff could plan for and manage the work flow of the project. Assignments were made in such a way as to attempt to spread the volume of work evenly over the six month period. We did not use teams to do the actual weeding because of the difficulty of adjusting schedules to accommodate team work, but we built a second opinion into the process by having the Collection Development Librarian review the material recommended for withdrawal by each librarian.

Each librarian was given an assignment form (see Figure 1) with a target month for the work and an instruction sheet (see Figure 2). In addition, one general training and discussion meeting was held concerning the project. During the month of their project assignment, librarians brought the materials they were recommending for withdrawal to a central location. The Collection Development Librarian reviewed the items brought down in the sort of quick and dirty approach recommended for the librarians. Approximately one-third of the material was returned to the collections after this second review. The percentage of materials to be retained varied with each subject and the expertise of the librarian doing the initial review, but the general percentage of one-third held true for the entire project. The review by the Collection Development Librarian was simplified because only the items considered candidates for withdrawal needed to be evaluated, and because the subject material could all be reviewed at one time. It was possible to see the patterns for each librarian and to compensate for extremes. Titles that needed further verification or investigation could be routed to classified staff for additional work and later returned for a final decision.

During this project, almost 2,000 shelves of monographs were reviewed to eliminate the obvious deadwood, and within a six month period, approximately 8,000 items were actually withdrawn from the collections. At the conclusion of the project, Access Services crews shifted the Dewey stacks to consolidate them and provide the needed space in the LC stacks where collection growth is occurring. Although the most obvious benefits of the project can be measured in the number of items withdrawn and the space gained for the more active pieces of the collections, other benefits can also be observed, if not exactly measured. These benefits include the added familiarity with older sections of the collections by public and technical services faculty. This knowledge is evident in collection development decisions as well as in reference work. There is also a shift in the understanding by our librarians of the six economic and philosophical factors mentioned in our opening remarks. The implications of our changing environment are becoming more evident to even our most conservative colleagues.

Another project is now being completed which looked at non-federal document serials (state, Canadian, United Nations, and

---

DEWEY MONOGRAPH WEEDING ASSIGNMENT FOR:

_____

SUBJECTS AND CALL NUMBER RANGES:

_____

_____

The general corresponding LC class numbers are:

_____

APPROXIMATE NUMBER OF MONOGRAPHIC SHELVES: _____

TIMELINE FOR ASSIGNMENT: _____ (do during this time

only and complete by the end of   _____)

YOUR ASSIGNMENT HAS DEWEY MATERIALS IN THE FOLLOWING LOCATIONS:

   Renne regular stacks   _____

      1st floor   _____   2nd floor   _____   3rd floor   _____

      4th floor   _____

   Renne storage on third floor   _____

   Classed documents collection, second floor   _____

   Creative Arts Library   _____

We will not deal with the items in Special Collections that are in Dewey. The oversize materials have all been reclassed to LC.
SPECIAL NOTES FOR YOUR SUBJECT AREAS:

Figure 1.

others) to determine the usefulness of keeping these often very short runs of titles for which there is little, if any, indexing access, and for which we do not hold primary responsibility. Certainly in areas of prime concern to our institutional mission, such as agriculture and technology, such titles would be kept. In many other areas, however, there are other appropriate libraries that have primary responsibility (formal or assumed) for titles. We have offered many items to other institutions to complete their runs for our collective good and have greatly cleaned up bibliographic records and the shelves. Access to

---

TO: Library Faculty

FR: Mary Bushing, Collection Development Officer

RE: Weeding of the Dewey monographs

THE PLAN: A "quick and dirty" weeding of the Dewey monographs. There are not enough resources at this time to allow us to do a title-by-title evaluation. We want to remove any items that obviously do not belong in The Libraries at MSU (e.g., we are not a "premiere" research institution and have limited numbers of graduate programs). Read the procedure and the attached assignment information. Give me a call or send me an E-Mail message if you have any questions either before you begin or as you work. I will be happy to try to accompany you to the shelves when you work on the weeding, if my schedule will allow it. If I am unable to work with you in the stacks, I will at least review all items pulled from the collection before they are withdrawn. The Dewey serials (including docs) will be evaluated in the reclass project. They do not need to be dealt with at this time. Monographic documents are to be considered for withdrawal.

PROCEDURE:
1. Read the MSU catalog to review what courses and degrees are offered that rely on materials in this division.
2. Browse a bit in the corresponding LC classification area (stacks, docs, and reference).
3. Take the index volume of *Books for College Libraries* (*BCL*) to the stacks with you to consult (if doubtful about a particular title or author). Please only keep the index while you are actually in the stacks. *BCL* is used daily in the collection development operation.
4. Take a book truck to the stacks with you and place on it any item you recommend for withdrawal.
5. Browse the collection shelf by shelf. Do not evaluate serial titles (including docs and monographic series), but do consider monographic documents.
6. Obvious items to be pulled:
    Duplicates, additional copies
    Superseded editions
    Older items, not used in 20 years (not in *BCL*)
    Textbooks
7. Obvious items which will need little attention include such things as the complete or collected works of an individual or chronological sets. It is likely that some of the individual monographs outside of the sets duplicate material in the sets and we might be able to withdraw the individual item because it is represented in the set. Each item needs to be evaluated on an individual basis.
8. Try to conclude each session in the stacks at some logical call number break, rather than right in the middle of a subject.
9. At the conclusion of each trip to the stacks move the books from your truck to the shelves and large cart in Meeting Room #2 (note signs to assist you) where they will be reviewed and moved on to the withdrawal process. Do not wait to move books to the room until you have a full cart or have finished your area.

Please ask me questions at any time.

The assessment assignments will be distributed by the end of February.

THANK YOU FOR YOUR CONTRIBUTION TO THIS PROJECT.

Figure 2.

material in the building is improved. Access to material in other collections is improved by our contribution to more complete holdings for a title in one location rather than many libraries with scattered holdings. When this weeding/evaluation project is completed, we will move on to another piece that can be accomplished, as the previous projects have been, with limited staff and in conjunction with regular workloads. We have found that the objection that weeding takes too much time is simply not true if projects are well planned and structured for very specific goals and within a limited time for completion.

As a result of our initial experience with the Dewey monograph project, a questionnaire (see Figure 3) was distributed to library faculty to help us better understand what previous training or experience each librarian had with weeding. We also wanted to know what insights they had gained from our project and what recommendations they might have for our organization or for other libraries.

We first asked when they had attended library school. Using the year ranges of 0-2, 3-5, 6-8, 9-11, and more than 12 years ago, we discovered an even distribution of attendance. It might also be noted here that of our twenty library faculty, seventeen different schools were attended for their library training, so a good cross-section of schools is represented. When asked the follow-up question—What was the total time spent in all of your library school classes on the topic of weeding/deselection?—all responded that it was less than ten percent of the time. Two respondents circled the choice of "None." Most mentioned that the course in which weeding was taught was called "Collection Development/Maintenance," although a few cited other courses in reference or library administration.

We then asked our faculty to summarize what was taught in their library school about weeding. We received a very brief response to this question. *All* of our librarians' responses reached a total length of ten sentences! In summary: discard outdated items unless they have historical value; be conservative, maintain awareness of potential research areas; never call it weeding, but deselection; last—copy policies and cooperation with other libraries; 80-20 rule, circulation life span, and obsolescence of information; monitoring collection growth and maintaining currency (space problems); very little—look

---

WEEDING QUESTIONNAIRE

Thank you for your participation in the weeding project. Now that you have finished your portion, please take a few minutes to fill in this questionnaire. It will be of great assistance to us, and the results will be shared. Thank you?

1. How long ago did you attend library school?
   _____ 0-2 yrs. _____ 3-5 yrs. _____ 6-8 yrs. _____ 9-11 yrs.
   _____ 12- yrs.

2a. What was the total time spent in all of your library school classes on the topic of weeding/deselection?

   _____ None _____ Less than 5% _____ 5-10% _____ 10-20%
   _____ 20-30% _____ more than 30%

   b. Approximate titles of courses in which weeding was mentioned?
   c. Please summarize what was taught concerning weeding?

3a Did you have experience in any other library with weeding?
   b. What kind of library? (i.e., academic, special, public, school)
   c. Describe what your experience was.

4. Approximately how much time per shelf did you spend in weeding your subject area here at MSU?

5. Before of during your project, did you:
   Look at other parts of the collection?
   Examine BCL or other bibliography?
   Consult our college catalog?

6a. Did your definition of the ideal MSU library collection change because of your participation in the weeding project?
   b. What insights did you gain?

7. For the subject you weeded, could you name three collection goals for MSU Libraries for the next two years?

8. Was the weeding project useful to you in your current position? How?

9. Was the weeding project useful to you in your future career goals? How?

10. What advice would you have for a colleague at another university starting work on a weeding project?

Figure 3.

at mission of library, item circulations, multiple copies, closed runs, and so forth; briefly mentioned that building size constraints and volume of materials made it sometimes necessary to weed; opposite of selection, but same principles; ALA Guide to Deselection promoted; and confirm policy and legal considerations, and get teaching faculty approval.

Despite the paucity of information given to library science students, all of our librarians, except two, had been expected to weed in previous positions and had experience weeding in another library before they worked on our project. That experience, along with our clear guidelines and suggestions for the project, appears to have formed the basis of their training.

Because of their participation in the weeding project, librarians indicated on the survey several positive things. Most were compelled to look at other parts of the collection, examine *BCL* (*Books for College Libraries*, 3rd ed.) or another bibliography, and review our curriculum offerings by examining the college catalog. Many thought that their definition of the ideal MSU library collection had changed because of participation in the weeding project. A majority felt that the project would be useful to them in their current position and in future career goals. Many also were able to develop useful recommendations for future purchases. Three future technical services projects were suggested involving other areas to review and target for retrospective conversion or reclassification.

The final question on the survey was: What advice would you have for a colleague at another university starting work on a weeding project? We share here some of their comments:

- Take it seriously, it's important.
- Divide collections into recognizable subject classes, by call numbers.
- Plan ahead, organize work flow, wear jeans, set restrictions and limitations as to what will be looked at and bring post-it notes to the stacks.
- Be merciless. I do not buy the argument for retaining obsolete materials (especially in the sciences) for potential historical interest. One handbook/text gives you an adequate reference for standard knowledge in a subject at the time of its publication. Pick the best one or two, then throw the rest away. Besides, I doubt that this kind of historical research is all that common.
- Wear old clothes (seriously!), look at the college catalog and don't be afraid to withdraw a book that is heavily used which is out of date and contains misinformation. Remember, new

books aren't necessarily better. Whenever possible, familiarize yourself with standard publishers, classic works, authors, etc., in the subject—then connections are easier to make.

- Learn what the university needs on hand. The most helpful tool for me was the college catalog. Another helpful thing was talking to departments in that subject area to hear what they are using and/or need to use in the future.
- Dig in—don't start with pre-conceptions.
- I would recommend following similar guidelines to what we have used.
- Allow lots of time and wear old clothes. Expect lots of interruptions if patrons recognize you, particularly if weeding near the reference desk!

Judging from these astute comments, despite their lack of formal library school training, we deem the project a success. Future weeding projects in our library now can build on that initial training. We would also argue that as a professional one is able to participate in weeding, given clear instructions and guidelines, even without prior bibliographic knowledge of a particular subject. Just do it!

After examining the results of our survey of MSU librarians who had participated in the weeding project, we were struck by the lack of formal training they had received in library school. We wondered whether that trend changed when library schools entered the 1990s, especially since collection management appears to be an increasingly important topic. A very simple survey was mailed to the fifty-nine American Library Association (ALA) accredited library schools in the United States and Canada. The survey asked two questions:

1.   Is weeding taught in your library school as a separate topic?

Yes _____   No _____

2.   If so please enter the name of the class and circle the approximate percent of time devoted to weeding in class.

Class Name: _____

Less than 5%   5-10%   10-20%   20-30%   More than 30%

We received an excellent response, with forty-four library school deans responding. We would like to take this opportunity to thank those deans and directors who took the time to complete the survey. We hope that what we have published here is useful information to them when planning future courses.

Four of the library schools said right out that they do not teach weeding. The remaining forty schools do teach weeding, always integrated into another class. No one responded that they teach an entire course just on weeding. As one might expect, the courses most frequently mentioned were Collection Management, Collection Development, and Acquisitions. A variety of others which integrated weeding into the course included: School Media Centers, Government Documents, Measurement and Evaluation of Library Services, Introduction to Information Science, Health Sciences Literature, Bibliography and Reference, Cataloging and Classification, and various other "special topics" courses such as Trends and Issues.

Within whatever class weeding was taught, the percentage of time was as follows. (Note: Some schools listed more than one class, which is why the following totals more than the forty-four schools that responded.)

Less than 5% = 35 classes
5-10%   = 20 classes
10-20%   = 5 classes
20-30%   = 1 class

Two schools did not respond to the percentage of time, and one clearly stated that it was one lecture out of fifteen. Several did note that the one class (usually collection development) in which it was covered was a mandatory or core course in their curriculum. The authors were also delighted to read a note on one survey that "weeding is taught in the section on evaluation, as well as in the section on writing a collection development policy."

We did not ask whether the library school curriculum was a one or two year program, but it is clear that given either system, weeding is being covered very little, if at all. One dean responded that it was taught and "mentioned in several others, more or less in passing."

It appears that even if a student takes a course in which weeding is covered, it is probably one hour of instruction in a typical three-credit, one semester course. Put another way, in a standard semester system with thirty-six credit-hours required for an MLS (master of library science) degree, hours of instruction upon graduation would be 1,620 classroom hours. Weeding would have been covered in one of those hours!

It does appear that the information we received from our faculty about their library school training remains accurate today. In fact, it might actually be worse, given that many schools no longer require core courses such as Collection Development that might cover weeding. In addition, many schools have expanded to two year programs but still responded that coverage of weeding was less than five percent.

There are many competing demands for what should or needs to be offered in a library school curriculum. It would be useful for schools to provide more than one hour on weeding, but that might not be possible. However, given that we were able to review training materials with our faculty in one hour, and the faculty spent approximately fifteen minutes weeding each shelf, it does seem that a lecture on weeding followed by a hands-on assignment would be possible. Moreover, given the positive experience of our faculty, it would be an excellent and worthwhile assignment. The majority of our faculty had been expected to weed collections in other positions, as well as at our institution. What better preparation for this important task than to have the hands on experience in library school rather than on a "real collection?" The guidelines of our project included checks and balances to prevent the novice from damaging our collection. How many libraries have a person on staff who can do that kind of teaching and mentoring? Unless weeding is taught, the problem will remain with us in two manifestations: Our collections will be weeded by librarians who have had no training in weeding or collection development, or, more likely, our collections will not be weeded at all since no one will even know how to begin. Our libraries cannot afford either scenario.

Based on our experience with this project, our investigation of the literature, the advice of our librarians, the responses from the library school deans, and our concern for the forces being brought to bear on academic librarianship, we agree with Richard M. Dougherty's comment in his editorial in 1989: "Maybe we should begin to rank libraries according to the number of volumes withdrawn along with the number of volumes added."[5] Until we really put to rest the concept that bigger is always better, we will continue to have librarians and institutions that think that more is better. We would prefer to believe that quality and ease of access are primary concerns of librarianship and that academic librarians are willing to accept and act on these principles.

NOTES AND REFERENCES

1.   Richard M.Dougherty, "Editorial: Ridding Collections of Deadwood," *Journal of Academic Librarianship* 15(March 1989): 3.

2.   S.K. Osheroff, "Team Weeding n a University Library," *College & Research Libraries News* 51(September 1989): 723-725.

3.   Lenore Clark, ed., *Guide to Review of Library Collections: Preservation, Storage, and Withdrawal*, Collection Management and Development Guides, No. 5 (Chicago: ALA Books, 1991).

4.   The review Area contains materials received as approval items, direct orders, gifts and selected state, federal and international documents as well as materials being evaluated for possible withdrawal or transfer to another collection area. Items are arranged in broad LC classifications. All instructional and library faculty are encouraged to examine these items to provide evalualtion comments and to apprise themselves of materials entering the collections.

5.   Dougherty, "Editorials," p. 3.

MAJOR MICROFORM SETS:
THE ALABAMA EXPERIENCE

Sue O. Medina, T. Harmon Straiton, Jr, and
Cecilia Schmitz

INTRODUCTION

After World War II, increased emphasis on research and the
establishment of new universities and colleges throughout the nation
resulted in unprecedented growth of library collections. As new funds
became available for collection building, librarians searched for
retrospective materials to establish new collections or correct
deficiencies in existing resources. Many needed items were
unobtainable. The few editions available through the out-of-print or
rare book market were often in poor condition or priced far beyond
what an institution could reasonably afford. One response to the
unavailability of historical materials was the acquisition of microform

Advances in Collection Development and Resource Management,
Volume 1, pages 79-100.
Copyright © 1995 by JAI Press Inc.
All rights of reproduction in any form reserved.
ISBN: 1-55938-213-9

collections consisting of desirable, hard-to-obtain, out-of-print materials. Improved microphotography technology enabled publishers to film an increasing variety of print materials and offer instant research collections for sale. These sets, usually organized within a subject or theme, offered several advantages. They preserved the intellectual content of the original source, books that often could not be used except under carefully controlled conditions due to their fragile condition. The acquisition of a set instantly enhanced a collection and corrected deficiencies in retrospective holdings. Scholars and students achieved on-campus access to materials that had been unavailable to them.

For all their advantages, inadequate bibliographic control of the items included in large sets was a major disadvantage. Frequently, but not always, microform sets were accompanied by indexes or other guides to assist the user seeking a specific title. Occasionally, catalog cards were provided so that the library catalog could reflect the individual holdings in the set. The general practice, however, was to publish a set without adequate accompanying bibliographic guides, indexes, or catalog records. If bibliographic access to individual items was desired, librarians were expected to search title-by-title for Library of Congress cards describing the original print item or to do original cataloging.

As early as 1940, inadequate bibliographic control of microforms was identified as a growing problem.[1] In 1961 the first of several studies addressing bibliographic control of microforms held and being acquired by libraries began to appear. A study sponsored by the Association of Research Libraries (ARL) was one the first to recommend a cooperative effort to catalog individual titles within sets. Another of this study's recommendations resulted in the establishment of the National Register of Microform Masters at the Library of Congress.[2] In 1969, Donald C. Holmes produced a second study which warned of serious problems with microforms while bibliographic control remained so inadequate.[3] Then in 1972, Felix Reichmann and Josephine M. Tharpe urged the Library of Congress to extend MARC records to include microforms and analytics. They also suggested a frequently updated COM index of all microform analytics.[4] No progress was made toward implementing either suggestion. Professional discussions of the problem continued and were reported in the library literature.

In the late seventies, solutions to the problems of bibliographic control for microforms began to appear. In 1979, University Microforms International (UMI), a major producer of sets, announced that it would begin cataloging analytics into OCLC.[5] This program, established primarily to provide UMI with better internal bibliographic control for its products and services, would benefit libraries struggling with the same need for adequate bibliographic records. Also in 1979, the Association of Research Libraries received a grant from the National Endowment for the Humanities to support a project to develop a plan for the "cooperative creation and dissemination of bibliographic records for titles in microform records."[6] ARL contracted with Richard Boss of Information Systems Consultants, Inc. (ISCI) to once again investigate issues and develop a plan for improving bibliographic access to materials (principally monographs) held in microform. Project activities included a review of the literature; investigation of the role of microform publishers, including compensation for publishers' catalog records; examination of changes in cataloging rules for microforms which during the project involved a controversy over rules for description; identification of issues (and obstacles) related to the entry of records into a bibliographic utility database; and the identification of an appropriate role for the utilities in a national cooperative cataloging program. A broadly-representative advisory group, interviews, and reactions to draft reports assisted ISCI in developing its recommendations.[7]

ARL endorsed the plan resulting from the ISCI study, obtained funding for the ARL Microforms Project, and in 1981, initiated work under the direction of Jeffrey Heynen. Emerging technology, principally online shared bibliographic databases, offered the ARL Microforms Project a substantial advantage for success. Richard Boss had found that some universities had already begun to enter records into OCLC; some duplication of effort existed; and some projects, begun with enthusiasm, had been abandoned. To improve bibliographic access for both libraries and micropublishers, the ARL Microforms Project encouraged the creation of machine-readable records—records which could serve a variety of internal purposes as well as the cooperative purposes of a shared database. Most important, the ARL Microforms Project provided a central focal point and leadership for a shared solution. It filled a much-needed coordinating role to identify sets with a high priority for cataloging and encouraged coordinated efforts to catalog these sets into a bibliographic utility. Equally important, the Project participants were often eligible for financial support through cataloging grants awarded by the U.S. Office of Education from the Higher Education Act (HEA) Title II-C program. Another tangible result of the ARL Microform Project was the establishment of a clearinghouse to collect and disseminate information on library policies relating to cataloging microform analytics, holdings of individual libraries, and the existing status of bibliographic control of specific sets. Further, the clearinghouse sought to identify individual library priorities for cataloging sets as well as interest in cooperative projects. By 1986, the ARL Microform Project had surveyed libraries nationwide, identified the ten sets ranked as the top priority for cataloging, and found that six of these sets were being cataloged with financial support from HEA Title II-C.[8]

The ARL Microforms Project also had as one of its goals the creation of machine-readable cataloging by the micropublishers. UMI had initiated its own program[9] and by 1986 was responsible for the cataloging of ten sets on OCLC.[10] In addition, Research Publications funded cataloging for its set, *Nineteenth Century Legal Treatises*. Libraries participating in microform cataloging projects cited the need for bibliographic control and user access as the principal reasons for considering such an expensive and time-consuming effort. Librarians involved in the ARL survey and cooperative cataloging projects were keenly aware of the importance of the bibliographic utilities to their efforts. Demand for machine-readable records grew as more libraries automated and offered online public access catalogs. Creating records in the online catalogs improved access to individual titles in sets and made it possible to obtain the bibliographic records for sets for local automated systems. OCLC established its Major Microforms Service to help meet this growing demand. The program encouraged cataloging projects by waiving some OCLC charges and made it possible for OCLC members to acquire cataloging for sets at a significant cost savings.

The development of "set-processing," compiling all records for a set to create catalog cards or a magnetic tape of records, was a valuable capability which had been identified as important in the objectives of the ARL Microforms Project. OCLC also began to maintain a list of sets being cataloged online, a necessary task that nonetheless duplicated the ARL Microforms Project clearinghouse, and in 1988 the latter was moved to OCLC. In 1984, OCLC could offer records for 12 sets and reported 9 sets in process. By September 1991, its Major Microforms Service Quarterly Update listed 79 available sets (or units within sets) and another 32 sets in the process of being cataloged. While this number is impressive, the total available machine-readable records is small compared to the number of titles in the collections available for purchase.

The approach of the Research Libraries Group (RLG) was substantially different from OCLC. During the ISCI planning project, the Research Libraries group expressed an interest in a cooperative cataloging program that would emphasize the content (perhaps subject or language) over the format. While cataloging for Early American Imprints was done on RLIN, the major contribution of RLIN has been the creation of an online union list of microform master negatives. This list is an invaluable aid to scholarship as microforms have become the primary medium to ensure preservation of resources that might otherwise disappear. The union list enables libraries to identify endangered items which have been filmed; thus, they can know immediately that they do not need to undertake costly preservation action of an item in hand.

MICROFORMS IN ALABAMA ACADEMIC LIBRARIES

A large portion of the nonprint resources held in Alabama libraries are microforms. Two factors contributed to the growth of these collections. First, the emphasis on research during the 1960s underscored the historical deficiencies in library collections. Because higher education in Alabama has never been adequately funded, deficiencies existed in the individual retrospective library collections. One effort to strengthen these collections was the addition of significant works collected into microform sets. Second, the 1960s was also a period during which several new institutions were created or expanded from extension centers. Microform collections seemed an ideal solution, almost instantly creating libraries for new institutions.

In 1984, the Network of Alabama Academic Libraries (NAAL) was established to coordinate resource sharing among the institutions offering graduate education. The Network initiated an ambitious resource sharing program to insure that students, faculty members, and other researchers in Alabama have access to all materials held in any of the academic libraries. Its first priority was online bibliographic access to total library holdings through OCLC. As work on the database progressed, several factors affected planning: major microform collections contained essential research materials that could never be acquired in the original format, the sets themselves had become expensive, and the lack of information about ownership of major sets and about the individual holdings within sets hampered their use. Because neither the bibliographic records for sets nor individual titles are in most tools created to support resource sharing, coordinated collection development and interlibrary loan were handicapped. At best, libraries could report gross numbers of "pieces" held, but could seldom report titles of sets held or specific items within sets. Without adequate information to develop a statewide plan to convert or create machine-readable records for individual titles held in microform, these materials would be under-utilized for research or possibly duplicated unnecessarily. Better finding aids for microforms would support the Network's programs to enhance research by developing collections cooperatively and sharing resources through interlibrary loan.

Another factor, not related to the Network's resource sharing program, was also important. Libraries with significant holdings in microform needed machine-readable records to support in-house library automation programs. This increasing importance of online catalogs coupled with the growing use of shared bibliographic databases for resource sharing hastened the need to create or convert bibliographic records to machine-readable format for individual titles in the microform sets held by Alabama libraries.

THE ALABAMA MICROFORMS PROJECT

The Network of Alabama Academic Libraries needed to identify, catalog, and publicize the availability of the substantial resources held in microform in its members. A creative solution to the Network's problem, the Alabama Microforms Project, was proposed by T. Harmon Straiton, Jr., Head of the Microforms and Documents Department, and G. Boyd Childress, Social Sciences Reference Librarian, of the Auburn University Libraries. The Alabama Microforms Project would identify major microform sets held by Alabama academic, special, and public libraries. This union list would meet the planning needs of NAAL and, once disseminated, increase access to microforms and support shared collection development, a significant NAAL program.

UNION LIST OF MICROFORM SETS

In 1986, NAAL, Auburn University Libraries, and the Alabama Public Library Service, the state library agency, cooperatively sponsored the union list. Academic, special, and public libraries with microform holdings were invited to contribute entries. Libraries were surveyed and provided data sheets to identify sets and holdings for each set (or parts of sets). Mr. Straiton researched missing data elements, and, where possible, verified the correct form of entry for the set. He also added information about indexes, bibliographies, or other guides which improved access to individual titles in a set. Suzanne Dodson's *Microform Research Collections: A Guide*[11] and the OCLC database were valuable resources for this task. The Alabama Public Library Service provided clerical support and entered the data into its computer. *Major Microform Sets Held in Alabama Libraries, A Union List and Guide*[12] was published by NAAL in 1988 and distributed to all contributing libraries. Additional copies were distributed to other academic libraries and regional public libraries in Alabama.

An important consideration in creating the union list was the development of parameters and standards to guide the participating libraries. The compiler, Harmon Straiton, in consultation with the sponsoring agencies, was authorized to make final decisions. Definitions for sets and the scope of collections to be included were prepared and distributed with a description of the purpose of the union list to Alabama libraries.

Definitions

Microform Collection or Set

A distinct group of publications, usually available as a complete set, sharing at least one of the following: (1) common subject, (2) time span, (3) common author (either personal or corporate), and (4) medium. Generally a microform collection or set stands alone as a separate title or titles and is comprised of monograph and/or serial titles; for example, *Early American Imprints*, First Series (Evans), a microprint edition of the complete text of every existent book, pamphlet, broadside, and so forth published in the United States from 1639 to 1800, *Index of American Design*, a vast collection covering every aspect of the decorative, folk, and popular arts; or the *Papers of Horatio Gates*, a collection of the papers of Gates.

Ready Reference Microform Collection

A distinct group of materials which can be used as an accessible source of answers to less research-oriented type questions. Examples include the *College Catalog Collection* on microfiche, a collection of most domestic and foreign postsecondary educational bulletins, and *Phonefiche*, a collection of telephone directories from various cities of varying sizes in the United States and a few selected foreign countries.

Significant Collection of Personal Papers

A distinct group of personal papers, manuscripts, reports, or correspondence of an individual or organization such as the *Complete Works of William Hazlitt* and the *Papers of the Women's League of Voters*.

Literary, Musical, Photographic, or Other Collected Works

A discrete collection of related materials such as *America, 1935-46: The FSA/OWI Photographs*, a collection of 87,000 captioned photographs of life in America, as well as *French Books Before 1600* which includes important fifteenth- and sixteenth-century printed books covering many subject areas.

Census Materials

Generally a microform set of the original manuscripts generated by a particular census such as the *Alabama Industrial Census of 1850*, the *Alabama State Census of 1855*, and the *Census of Population, 1910*.

Monographic Series of Research Significance

A discrete collection of monographs such as *American Architectural Books*, a collection of 939 titles pertaining to architecture and held by the Avery Library of Columbia University, and *Early English Books, Series I, 1475-1640* which includes the first book published in England as well as nearly all of the 26,500 titles listed in A.W. Pollard and G.R. Redgrave's *Short-Title Catalogue*.

Serial Series of Research Significance

A unique collection of various serial publications covering a particular time period or subject. Examples are *American Periodicals, Series II, 1800-1850*, a comprehensive collection of 923 serial publications including virtually all of the significant magazines of the period; and the *"Little Magazines" Series 1889-1972: Selected Short-Run Cinema Periodicals* which includes the entire runs of 25 magazines held in the archives of the British Film Institute that are frequently identified in indexes, bibliographies, and so forth but are seldom held by a particular library.

Reference Titles

Collections of research/reference publications which have intrinsic importance or a close relationship to other microform sets included in *Major Microform Sets Held in Alabama Libraries, A Union List and Guide.* Examples include *Microfiche Concordance to Old English*, a collection of 412 microfiche pertaining to English literature from the time period ca. 450-1100; and *Bibliography of American Women*, a major research tool containing 50,000 titles that enable scholars and historians to gain greater insight, accuracy and breath in their study of women in American life.

The project initially defined a major microform set as containing five reels or more and a major microfiche set as having twenty-five sheets or more. These limitations were designed to make the first union list a more manageable project. A number of participating libraries expanded the definitions and submitted entries for titles consisting of a single bibliographic entity, a single reel, or a few microfiche sheets. Usually, these had been produced locally to preserve materials related to Alabama such as scrapbooks of newspaper clippings or the papers of individuals or families from Alabama. These entries were evaluated and those that were unique and which also offered research potential were included.

A staggering number of titles are distributed by the federal government as a part of the Federal Depository Library System. Because finding tools exist for federal publications, a concerted effort was made to include only those with high research value to a large segment of library users.

Format for Entries

Entries in *Major Microform Sets Held in Alabama Libraries, A Union List and Guide* include the following data fields: main entry/title, publisher, format, content, index/bibliography, and holdings. Data for any of these fields are missing only if an extensive effort failed to determine the necessary information.

Main Entry/Title of the Microform Collection. The compiler selected the best record and established the form of entry. In most instances, the AACR2 format was used after verification on the OCLC database.

Publisher of the Microform Collection. The majority of sets were commercially prepared. Similar sets produced by different publishers were treated as separate entries to ensure that citations, indexing, etc. prepared for a specific set could be used to facilitate interlibrary loan. There are a number of entries for micromaterials which had been filmed by agencies such as the Alabama Department of Archives and History and the Birmingham Public Library. While nominally outside the scope of the union list, these were included because of their value to research throughout the state.

Format. The format of the materials was important for interlibrary loan purposes. The kind of equipment available in a local library could determine whether or not an interlibrary loan request would be placed. Entries were designated microcard (3 x 5 inch, opaque), Microprint (6 x 9 inch microprint, opaque), microfilm (16mm or 35mm, positive or negative), microfiche (4 x 6 inch, positive or negative), and ultrafiche (4 inch, positive or negative). In each case, the number of units (sheets or rolls) was included, if known.

Content. A concerted effort was made to include copious content or scope notes; however, in those cases where the title of the microform set clearly indicated its contents, such notes were not included. The note also indicated the arrangement of the material in the set (e.g., volumes and their contents, microfilm reels or microfiche sheets and their contents, chronologically, alphabetically by author or title, geographically, etc.).

Index/Bibliography. One of the most time-consuming activities was identifying the various tools which had been created to facilitate access to the contents of the sets. Listings of these indexes and bibliographies have not been consistently compiled. A number of these are located within the microformatted materials. Some are not separate publications but are distributed to purchasers of the sets. Whenever possible, a complete bibliographic citation was provided.

Sixteen public and private college and university libraries, one large public library, the state library agency, and one special library submitted 989 titles with holdings information. Of these, 711 met the criteria for inclusion in the first union list. A revised, expanded, and enlarged edition of the union list was completed in 1991. It contained 1,107 titles, and the scope notes as well as the related the number of indexes and bibliographies were greatly expanded. Contributing libraries increased to nineteen.

In addition to the three-volume paper edition of the union list, it was made available in an electronic version with WordPerfect, Microsoft Word, or ASCII formats provided to contributing libraries. The electronic version enhanced keyword searching of the entire bibliographic entry and, hence, provided greater access to the information in the publication.

Major Microform Sets Held in Alabama Libraries, A Union List and Guide met its initial goal: to identify the sets held by Alabama libraries. More important, it spawned additional activities to expand scholarly access to microform materials. These included "tagging" bibliographic records in the OCLC database with holding libraries' symbols, encouraging local libraries to acquire machine-readable bibliographic records for various microform sets for loading into their own online public access catalogs, and planning to convert the union list to the OCLC union listing subsystem.

BIBLIOGRAPHIC RECORDS FOR
MICROFORM SETS HELD BY NAAL MEMBERS

The goal of the Network of Alabama Academic Libraries is to make the total academic library resources accessible to students and scholars throughout Alabama. Bibliographic records for all monographs and serials held by NAAL members were added to OCLC to support resource sharing. Adding these records was a relatively easy and affordable project. Adding records for the wealth of information owned in microform represented a huge, expensive, perhaps impossible, undertaking. The publication of *Major Microform Sets Held in Alabama Libraries, A Union List and Guide*, helped NAAL manage planning for this effort. It was a fortuitous coincidence that OCLC initiated its Major Microforms Service just as NAAL began to seek sources of machine-readable records for microform sets. An important benefit of the Service is the savings it represents in obtaining catalog records for a microform set. Records purchased through OCLC cost less than $0.20 per record, a huge savings over title-by-title cataloging.[13] These records also offer a time savings as large numbers of records loaded into a local database give almost instant bibliographic access to thousands of "new," or previously "hidden," works. Acquiring records from OCLC also adds the holding symbol for libraries owning the sets to the online catalog, enabling libraries to share these resources. In 1987, the Network included the acquisition of records for microform sets as a shared funding initiative in its program to build a statewide online database. The Network paid the OCLC charge to display the library's holding symbol online; the local library funded the cost of the magnetic tape of the records for loading into its local system. In 1988, the Network paid $0.17 per record to set 161,072 holding symbols. These locations represented 64,881 individual bibliographic records held in fourteen microform sets. Local libraries acquired the magnetic tape of records (at a rate that varied from $0.022 to $0.046 per record depending on the number of records in the set) to add these into their online public access catalogs.[14] The Statewide Database Program to acquire machine-readable records continues, and NAAL has added nearly 300,000 holding symbols through the OCLC Major Microform Service. Thus, nearly 150,000 individual titles included in twenty-seven microform sets display Alabama libraries' holding symbols on OCLC. NAAL members agree to provide these materials (either the microform or a printed copy from the microform) to other NAAL members via interlibrary loan; most will also lend them to other OCLC libraries. Ironically, one of the very first interlibrary loan requests from an out-of-state library sought to borrow a title included in a set that it owned. NAAL librarians routinely check holdings attached to the bibliographic record of a set and often find this is true; evidence that local bibliographic access to titles held in microform continues to a problem. Acquiring machine-readable records through the OCLC Major Microform Service, an affordable solution to improving bibliographic control of microform titles, should be explored by automated libraries.

Discussions were also held with the state library agency staff to explore the benefits of adding the microform set records to the state's union catalog, ALICAT, which is distributed in microfiche and CD-ROM to public libraries and other libraries contributing records. Unfortunately, OCLC denied permission to add the major microform set records to ALICAT. Including these records in the union catalog would have expanded access to the materials held in microform to users outside the academic community.

ORIGINAL CATALOGING OF MICROFORM SETS

The first edition of the union list identified 711 major microform sets held in the state. Bibliographic records for only twenty-seven sets could be acquired through OCLC. Therefore, original cataloging for the remaining sets had to be considered if individual titles were to be made more accessible. Because of the expense of original cataloging, the Network adopted a policy supporting the purchase of the online holdings symbol display for major microform sets as they became available from OCLC and the cost of tape loading into OCLC any machine-readable records obtained from other sources. At the same time, it actively encouraged, but did not fund, original cataloging projects. At Auburn University Libraries, several sets were evaluated for their importance to Alabama scholars. Working with librarians at the University of Alabama, two sets were identified as high priority for cataloging: *Confederate Imprints, 1861-1865* and *French Revolutionary Pamphlets*. Because most Alabama academic institutions support graduate education in history and most offer concentrations in American and Southern history, the 13,000 items in these two sets are important to scholarship throughout the state.

Confederate Imprints, 1861-1865 includes over 6,000 source documents critical to the study of Southern history. With the acquisition of this collection, almost any library becomes a major Civil War research center. The publications cover a continuum from religious tracts to the journal of Mississippi secession and represent the great majority of books and miscellaneous publications published in the Confederacy. Increased ease of identification and availability of so comprehensive and valuable source of material is important for research in the history of the Old South, the Confederacy, and the Civil War.

French Revolutionary Pamphlets presents materials documenting the evolution of critical thought in democratic theory. The bulk of the collection covers the years 1787 to 1800, although a few pamphlets were published in slightly earlier or later years. The period of the National (Constituent) Assembly is especially well represented. Many facets of the revolutionary era—political, religious, cultural, financial—are illuminated for the scholar by these contemporary materials. While a large number of the items are documents printed by order of executive bodies, at least half of the collection is comprised of pamphlets arguing either support or opposition to reforms of the period.

The Network of Alabama Academic Libraries coordinated development of a proposal for submission to the U.S. Office of Education for funding from the Higher Education Act Title II-C to catalog these two sets. Auburn University served as the lead institution and fiscal agent for the project. This original cataloging project completed the necessary name and subject authority work as well as assured access for scholars throughout the nation to the individual title records. Librarians at Auburn University Libraries cataloged *Confederate Imprints, 1861-1865*. Librarians at the University of Alabama cataloged *French Revolutionary Pamphlets*, their task assisted by previous work during which most of the authority work needed to catalog the individual titles had been completed. Over a three-year period, HEA II-C provided $269,564 to complete original cataloging for these two sets. Other libraries that own the sets can now acquire the machine-readable records from OCLC for loading into their own automated systems, thus improving local access to their own resources.

Activities for the cataloging project were divided between the two universities. Auburn University Libraries, as grant recipient and fiscal agent, subcontracted with the University of Alabama Libraries for cataloging *French Revolutionary Pamphlets*. The project was integrated into its technical services department and competed with existing staff. Prior to the project, the University of Alabama Libraries had produced analytics for the set; this enabled the University to complete its cataloging in the first two years of the project.

Cataloging the *Confederate Imprints, 1861-1865* Microfilm Set

Auburn University Libraries managed the project as a separate activity with special project staff and, due to space limitations, less than permanent or ideal locations. In December 1988, Cecilia Schmitz was appointed project cataloger. She brought excellent skills to the project as a result of her previous experience in a similar activity to catalog the major set, *Goldsmiths'-Kress Library of Economic Literature*, at Texas A&M University. Consequently, no additional training was needed and the project could begin immediately upon her arrival at Auburn. Other staff employed for the project included a Library Assistant and, after several months into the project, two student assistants. Existing library faculty and staff contributing to the project included the Head of Microforms and Documents and the Head of Cataloging.

Auburn University Libraries had just begun a new addition to the Ralph Brown Draughon Library when the grant was awarded. No space was available in the current and overcrowded Cataloging Department to house the new unit. An office with cataloging work space was created in a hallway. Its remote location, a floor below the Cataloging Department, required the duplication of some cataloging tools. The grant and Auburn University Libraries provided necessary equipment: two NOTIS terminals, a Telex for transferring OCLC records into NOTIS, a microfilm reader/printer, a printer, and one OCLC M310 which was chained via an "extended distance" cable to other OCLC terminals in other parts of the library. This chaining caused equipment problems and a significant amount of down-time during the first year and a half of the three year project. Downtime was not limited to just the project office, on one occasion the project's M310's cable resulted in loss of a major part of the OCLC system.

As work on the library addition and subsequent renovation of existing space progressed, the project was disrupted twice to change its location. A move in the second year obtained a quieter location which did not suffer as many power interruptions from construction activities. During the third year, the unit moved with the Cataloging Department into the new quarters for the Department. Asynchronious OCLC work stations resulted in almost no downtime. Other improvements were the ability to toggle between NOTIS and OCLC on one work station and the replacement of the Telex system by GTO.

In spite of space constraints, construction disruption, and poor locations, the project developed an efficient work flow. Early in the project, it became apparent that cataloging in batches would be more efficient than cataloging item by item. The following 16-step process was developed in which one task was completed for many records at a time.

1. Photocopy necessary information (holdings, title page(s), imprint, etc.) and attach photocopies to cataloging workform to make packet: Student Assistant, Library Assistant;
2. Search item in OCLC: Student Assistant, Library Assistant
3. Initial cataloging of item: Library Assistant;
4. Create record in OCLC Save file and attach printout to packet: Student Assistant, Library Assistant;
5. Final cataloging of item: Cataloger;
6. Establish authority records: Cataloger, Library Assistant;
7. Add authority records to NOTIS: Library Assistant;
8. Revision of Save file record: Library Assistant;
9. Initial review of cataloging: Cataloger;
10. Final review of cataloging: Library Assistant;
11. Correct records in Save file: Library Assistant;
12. Search OCLC for duplicate record, and update holdings for FEI: Library Assistant;
13. Transfer record to NOTIS: Library Assistant;
14. Revise NOTIS record, if necessary, for local use: Student Assistant;
15. Record statistics: Student Assistant;
16. File cataloging workform packet: Student Assistant.

With extensive training and experience gained on the project, the student assistants were able to handle all photocopying, the initial OCLC search, input into the OCLC Save file, and the final revision of the NOTIS record—addition of local call number and fixing the item-holdings screen.

Over time, the Library Assistant became adept at cataloging and was able to complete as much as 99 percent of each record. Use of

NOTIS was a valuable asset which helped insure consistency in cataloging decisions, subject assignments, and name authority work. Also, its subject and keyword searching capabilities greatly facilitated quality control.

In the first year, 1,572 items were cataloged. Increased staff efficiency and less equipment downtime enabled the project to catalog 2,236 items in the second year. In the third and last year, 2,158 items were cataloged. With the project's conclusion in November 1991, a total of 5,966 records had been cataloged for *Confederate Imprints*.

When the project was conceived, it was anticipated that a substantial number of records for the print items would exist in the OCLC database. A high "hit rate" would have facilitated authority work and cataloging. In reality, 69 percent of the records required original cataloging. The project found similar cataloging records for 31 percent of the items; primarily DLC records for materials in different formats cataloged prior to 1940. Only seven records were for microform materials. The majority of the items in the set were monographs; however, the set also included 672 scores, 28 maps, 13 serials, 1 greeting card, and 1 postcard. The majority of the items, approximately 2,288, were published in Virginia with a large number from South Carolina (822 items) and Georgia (740). Few items in the set were concerned with individual battles; most of the general orders were policy oriented. Finally, users with access to the original items could surmise the progress of the war by the declining quality of paper. Eight items (including a copy of Charles Dickens' *Great Expectations*) were printed on wallpaper.

The microfilm cataloging project was successful in meeting the objectives set out in the initial grant proposal. Equally important, the project was a successful experience for Auburn University Libraries. Although handicapped by construction during the library expansion, the project was completed a month earlier than originally scheduled. Credit for this achievement accrues to a highly motivated staff at Auburn University Libraries, excellent project staff, a well-equipped work space, and good organization for work flow. While the physical separation from the Cataloging Department could have created additional problems, the staff were able to function collaboratively. The microform cataloging unit functioned with a great deal of autonomy once its initial performance was reviewed.

Finally, everyone associated with the project was able to adapt quickly to change and maintain project efficiency.

THE FUTURE

In 1991, OCLC announced that its Union Listing Subsystem could be used for formats other than serials. Plans were being made for an updated edition of the union list and the online union listing seemed to be a effective way to improve access. Converting the database to OCLC would insure more up-to-date holdings information than could be provided through the printed edition. NAAL allocated funds for the conversion of the union list records and holdings into OCLC, and Auburn University Libraries agreed to serve as the union listing agent to create the online union list. Auburn University Libraries would select the best OCLC record and create the Local Data Records (LDRs) for each set already in the union list. After this initial project, input would be decentralized. NAAL members acquiring additional holdings would create or revise their own LDRs; those acquiring sets not in the existing union list would add the bibliographic record and their holdings to the union list. Unfortunately, the announcement of availability of union listing for nonserial formats preceded software development at OCLC to distinguish between formats for off-line products. The current software cannot distinguish a union list record by format; a serial microform record input as a union listing record will appear in any union listing off-line product in which a library participates. Because the state library agency distributes the Alabama Union List of Serials (AULS) in microfiche and on CD-ROM, any serial microform LDR created by a library participating in AULS would be included in the AULS off-line products. The result would be to degrade the excellent quality of the AULS database. In addition, the state library agency would have to pay to acquire off-line records that it did not create and did not want. While OCLC recognizes the need for a programming change, no date has been scheduled for this change. As a result, the enticing opportunity to create an online union catalog of microforms cannot be utilized.

NAAL will fund the acquisitions of set holdings as new records become available through the OCLC Major Microform Service and will fund the cost of tape loading into OCLC any machine-readable records obtained by its members from other sources.[15] It has no plans to pay for original cataloging, leaving the decision to catalog microform records and the necessary financing to its members. The possibility of developing another proposal for funding from HEA has been temporarily suspended. The current economic downturn has resulted in retrenchment at all Alabama academic institutions and none can initiate a major cataloging project in the midst of freezes on filling positions.

The Network has funded acquisition of major microform sets as part of its Statewide Collection Development Program. In 1990, its Research Support grant program, which funds acquisition of materials unique to the members collective holdings, supported the acquisition of twenty-six periodical backfiles in microform selected from *Black Journals;*[16] *Black Biographical Dictionaries, 1790-1950;*[17] the then-available units of *Black Literature, 1827-1940;*[18] Part 1 (1924-1975) of the *Schomberg Clipping File;*[19] and *The Eighteenth Century.*[20] In 1991, awards for this program demonstrated reluctance to support purchase of sets which could not be utilized statewide for lack of bibliographic access. The Network received proposals to acquire several major sets, but Research Support awards were only approved for the acquisition of three microform units of the *National Criminal Justice Reference Service*[21] which was integrated into a proposal with the broader scope of Forensic Science. The number of sets held in the state continues to grow while the Network struggles to improve bibliographic access to the wealth of publications contained in them. Without a stronger commitment by publishers to provide machine-readable records with their sets and an increased effort to catalog existing sets, the goal of a database offering bibliographic access to the total information resources held by our libraries may never be achieved.

NOTES AND REFERENCES

1. Herman H. Fussler, "Microfilm and Libraries." In *The Acquisition and Cataloging of Books*, edited by William M. Randall. (Chicago: University of Chicago Press, 1940).

2. Wesley Simonton, "The Bibliographical Control of Microforms" *Library Resources and Technical Services* 6(Winter 1962): 29-40.

3. Donald C. Holmes,*Determination of User Needs and Future Requirements for a Systems Approach of Microform Technology* (Washington , DC: Association of Research Libraries, 1969).

4. Felix Reichmann and Josephine M. Tharpe. *Bibliographic Control of Microforms.* (Westport, CT: Greenwood Press, 1972).

5. Linda K. Hamilton, "UMI and the OCLC Option." *Microform Review* 10(Spring 1981): 79-83.

6. Richard W. Boss, *Cataloging Titles in Microform Sets: Report of a Study Conducted in 1980 for the Association of Research Libraries by Information Systems, Inc.* (Washington, DC: Association of Research Libraries, 1983): 73.

7. Richard. W. Boss, *Cataloging Titles in Microform Sets.*

8. Martin D. Joachim, "Recent Developments in the Bibliographic Control of Microforms." *Microform Review* 15(Spring 1986): 74-86.

9. Hamilton, "UMI and the OCLC Option."

10. Joachim, "Recent Developments."

11. Suzanne Dodson, *Microform Research Collections: A Guide* (Westport, CT: Microform Review, 1978).

12. *Major Microform Sets Held in Alabama Libraries, A Union List and Guide.* Comp. and ed. T. Harmon Straiton, Jr. and G. Boyd Childress. (Montgomery: Network of Alabama Academic Libraries, Alabama Commission on Higher Education, 1988).

13. During 1981 to 1983, the University of Utah cataloged 9,474 records for Landmarks of Science at an average cost per title of $25.33, including personnel benefits, purchase of equipment and supplies, and administrative overhead.

14 In an exception to this policy, NAAL does not fund the acquisition of records for sets held in micro-opaque cards. NAAL members are reluctant to lend these; and most libraries, unless they own micro-opaque sets, do not have the equipment necessary to use them.

15. As of September 1991.

16. *Black Journals.* (Westport, CT: Greenwood Press, 1970-75).

17. *Black Biographical Dictionaries, 1790-1950.* (Cambridge, England: Chadwyck-Healey). The OCLC Major Microform Service has included this set in its list of "Sets in Progress."

18. *Black Literature, 1827-1940.* (Cambridge, England: Chadwyck-Healey. Segment 1, Fall 1989).

19. *Schomberg Clipping File.* (Cambridge, England: Chadwyck-Healey).

20. *The Eighteenth Century.* (Woodbridge, CT: Research Publication. An ongoing set. Combined funding from the University of Alabama at Birmingham (UAB) and the Network of Alabama Academic Libraries enabled UAB to acquire units available to date.

21. *National Criminal Justice Reference Service.* (Washington, DC: U.S. Department of Justice, National Institute of Justice. Funding from NAAL enabled University of Alabama at Birmingham to complete its holdings for all available units. Bibliographic access to items in this set is provided by SuDocs No. J 28.22:972-984.

STATEWIDE COOPERATION TO IMPROVE ACADEMIC LIBRARY RESOURCES:

THE ALABAMA EXPERIENCE

Sue O. Medina and William C. Highfill

BACKGROUND

The reality that traditionally defines Alabama is a highly politicized arena in which segments of higher education, university systems, and individual institutions compete in an annual struggle for very limited state resources. A regressive tax structure, very low property tax rates, and the absence of home rule for raising local taxes prevent adequate funding for services at all levels of government. Few incentives encourage or reward cooperation; funding success is tied more closely to political acumen than to state need. With this background, Alabama would seem to be among the least likely of states in which a cooperative network for academic libraries would emerge.

Advances in Collection Development and Resource Management,
Volume 1, pages 101-137.
Copyright © 1995 by JAI Press Inc.
All rights of reproduction in any form reserved.
ISBN: 1-55938-213-9

In the late 1970s, Alabama faced a crisis in funding while its leaders were grappling with issues related to the quality of higher education, the growing duplication of academic programs, and the need for the state to utilize its financial resources more effectively. Academic librarians responded to these widely discussed concerns by emphasizing the library as a measure of quality in higher education and suggesting cooperation as a means to utilize resources more effectively. An assessment of libraries, published in 1983, reported that the library resources of Alabama institutions offering graduate education were woefully inadequate.[1] *Cooperative Library Resource Sharing Among Universities Supporting Graduate Study in Alabama* documented the facts that Alabama libraries lacked sufficient resources to support the existing graduate instructional and research programs of their parent institutions and demonstrated that they lagged far behind their peers elsewhere in the nation in book and serial holdings, staffing, facilities, use of technology, and access to external resources. The report's recommendations found widespread support among the institutions and led to the establishment of an academic consortium in 1984 to coordinate a statewide program for sharing library resources supporting graduate education and research.

The Network of Alabama Academic Libraries (NAAL) was organized in 1984 and initially funded with assessments to its members. The Network's voting membership included the state's coordinating body for higher education, the Alabama Commission on Higher Education (ACHE), and publicly- and privately-supported academic institutions offering graduate degrees. In addition, other libraries with research-level collections were encouraged to join as cooperative but nonvoting members. The first activities of the Network were to establish priorities for the recommendations in *Cooperative Library Resource Sharing*, develop a strategic plan, and lobby the state legislature for funding. NAAL received its first state appropriation in fiscal year 1984-85.

Once NAAL began to function as a formal organization, it faced three issues that could have threatened its success: the lack of a tradition of collaboration among its participants, a need to accommodate both the homogeneity and diversity of the institutions, and a need to address the expectations of the state's leaders that

NAAL would solve or significantly reduce very serious, long-term deficiencies in library resources and services.

Overcoming Lack of Collaboration Among Participants

Governance of NAAL rests in its Advisory Council, a body composed of a representative of each member institution.[2] Voting representatives to the first Council included university presidents, academic deans, and librarians. Like any new organization, its participants had to develop effective working relationships if it were to succeed.

Because the political environment of Alabama had seldom rewarded cooperation, representatives of the academic institutions that formed NAAL had little experience in working collaboratively. Presidents of public universities had had some experience working together through the Council of Presidents, an advisory group to the Alabama Commission on Higher Education. The Commission, however, is legally responsible for planning among only publicly-supported senior colleges and universities. Consequently, member-ship on ACHE's advisory groups was limited to that constituency. Since the future network would include privately-supported institutions, the presidents of these schools worked with the Council of Presidents to devise the plans and governance structure for the Network. This extended group of presidents worked together for about a year to formulate the NAAL constitution and bylaws and to lobby for funding of the consortium.

The Council of Librarians, another ACHE advisory group representing the publicly-supported institutions, had conducted the statewide library assessment noted earlier. Librarians from privately-supported institutions that were potential participants were invited to work with the Council of Librarians members to plan the Network. This group translated the recommendations of *Cooperative Library Resource Sharing* into a workable program and set priorities for their implementation.

NAAL's first Advisory Council drew its membership from both ACHE groups, the presidents and the librarians. Each had worked through its own Council, but these individuals had not functioned extensively in a group drawn from both Councils. The composition,

members, and size of the NAAL Advisory Council made frequent
meetings to discuss issues facing the new network difficult. As the
NAAL program evolved, members would be expected to develop and
adopt policies dealing with complex issues and relationships. It was
important that Council members be provided with substantial
background information to insure that decisions would best meet the
statewide mission of NAAL, but the amount of time available for
Council meetings did not permit lengthy introductions or substantial
briefings before votes had to be taken. To meet the need for informed
discussion in policy development, working committees were
appointed and charged with developing recommendations for
consideration by the full Council.

The Collection Development Committee was the first standing
committee appointed for the NAAL program. Its membership was drawn
from institutional representatives and, importantly, from librarians with
specialized knowledge who could lend expertise in planning this activity.

Philosophical and theoretical discussions about the nature of
Alabama's academic libraries and current trends in the rapidly
emerging field of cooperative collection development marked the
early meetings of the Collection Development Committee.
Thoughtful white papers with equally reflective responses were
distributed for consideration and discussion. This committee set a
standard for all future NAAL deliberations: a high level of
professionalism, discussion supported by research and logic, a focus
on statewide needs, and an absence of parochial agendas.

As Committee members learned to work together effectively, so
too the Advisory Council had to build its collaborative model. The
new Committee structure did not remove the necessity for the Council
to decide complex issues affecting its members. Extensive committee
discussions insured that any of its members would understand an
issue and its background. Despite that, it proved difficult to explain
such things as the complexities and benefits of a policy
recommendation in the limited time available for a full Advisory
Council meeting. Widespread distribution of white papers and
minutes of Committee meetings did not completely insure that each
member had sufficient background for informed voting. The two
meetings held during each year did not provide the Advisory Council
the time for orientation to and discussion of issues.

A continuing series of annual three-day planning retreats at which all NAAL programs are reviewed and all current proposals discussed became the solution. The retreat is held at a beach resort, off-season when the rates and distraction levels of sun and surf are low. Retreat ambiance is deliberately casual to encourage easy and open interaction. Ample time is scheduled for discussion of each issue and time is allowed for small groups to form and work. No votes are taken, and members are encouraged to explore alternate solutions and suggestions thoroughly. Representatives new to NAAL receive a subtle orientation to the democratic norms that direct NAAL's deliberations. By the end of the retreat, participants have reviewed thoroughly the background and nuances of issues presented later for decisions at the annual business meeting during which the NAAL program for the year is adopted.

After working together for ten years, NAAL members have forged a culture that stimulates democratic discussion. All ideas and suggestions are received and given full consideration. Only three current voting representatives were members of the first Advisory Council, but newer members have embraced the vision for statewide academic library cooperation that was first articulated in the early 1980s.

Accommodating Homogeneity and Diversity of Participants

Library consortia members choose their partners for myriad reasons. Each model offers advantages and disadvantages for activities such as cooperative collection development. Multitype systems cite the benefit of increased diversity of available materials. Institutions with similar missions may, of necessity, duplicate more of their core materials. Unique materials they hold, however, may correlate more closely with the needs of their specific users.

On the surface, all NAAL members are homogeneous. All are accredited publicly- or privately-supported institutions offering graduate education. With one exception, all offer four years of study leading to a baccalaureate degree. The advantages of its members possessing a high degree of homogeneity are manifest in their sharing common problems and a common language. Publicly-supported institutions in the consortium also share the poverty of insufficient state funding. NAAL's private institutions echo a corresponding lack of adequate financial support found all too frequently in a tuition- and endowment-dependent environment. NAAL homogeneity is underscored by the findings of the assessments of the early 1980s: All suffered the deficiencies identified in the study; none was adequate by the measures used for evaluation.

This appearance of homogeneity is deceptive. A closer examination reveals significant diversity. Institutional autonomy has resulted in curricula that are different, especially at the graduate level, because each institution is able to define its own mission and programs. While there is considerable replication of academic program titles, scholarly emphasis of a given program may differ markedly from others with a similar title. Diversity among the state-supported institutions is gradually increasing, a result of a policy implemented in the early 1980s requiring ACHE approval of new academic programs. This helps prevent unnecessary duplication. Declining enrollment also eliminates some existing programs.

The varying sizes of NAAL members also increase their diversity. Members include medium-sized comprehensive universities at one end of the spectrum and a very small single program school at the other. Student populations range from 22,000 to 300 head count students. Library collection sizes are from 1.2 million to 3,400 volumes. One institution offers only one graduate program; another supports nearly two hundred.

NAAL institutions also attract diverse student bodies. Institutions with open enrollment policies may attract the majority of their students from primarily rural, educationally-disadvantaged backgrounds. These students may require more remedial work. On more selective campuses, students may be better prepared academically. Three members are historically black institutions which cope with the traditional problems of economically-disadvantaged students for whom attending college may not be an easily achieved goal.

Within any large group, potential exists for subgroups to share goals that differ from those of other members. For NAAL, easily identifiable contrasts such as large-small, urban-rural, or public-private could be the basis for defining such a subgroup.

Throughout NAAL's history, the state has been embroiled in a lawsuit between the historically black institutions (plaintiffs) versus the Alabama Commission on Higher Education and several predominately white institutions (defendants). This adversarial relationship of the court case has not affected at all the relationship between the representatives of any of these schools as they work within NAAL. A group norm established early in NAAL history stresses that issues will be considered on a statewide basis. Potential benefits to be realized by all of the members, not those which accrue to type or size of member institution, are always paramount.

Homogeneity resulting from a common background and similar problems contributes positively to policy development. The state basis for organization insures a shared political orientation. This facilitates agreement upon a vision to improve statewide academic library resources and services. Diversity requires members to consider numerous alternates to insure that actual implementation of a policy will have the desired outcome for each member. Policy formulation and program implementation may, at times, appear to evolve slowly as a result of that process. Nonetheless, it affords each member's representative the opportunity to analyze proposed options from a perspective that not only accounts for the distinctive attributes of that school but also recognizes that the intent and outcome of NAAL policies and programs support the statewide library and information needs of Alabama.

Addressing Unrealistic Expectations

Leaders of higher education supporting NAAL at its inception expected it to correct deficiencies accumulated for decades. Some senior-level administrators and legislators assumed that NAAL would immediately end duplication of library resources and save money. Although no time frame was established for meeting the lofty goals presented in *Cooperative Library Resource Sharing*, most leaders expected a quick return on investment. Thus, the fledgling network faced the difficulties of demonstrating accomplishments early in its history and, simultaneously, overcoming the unrealistic expectations of reducing unnecessary holdings replication and saving financial resources.

Discussion of the duplication issue was intense and frequent. The Advisory Council reviewed the politics of academic program duplication in higher education while the Collection Development Committee studied the need for collection management information that would enable it to assess holdings replication accurately. Ultimately, NAAL agreed that each library should provide the core collection necessary to meet the basic information needs of students and faculty of the institution, regardless of how many academic programs were replicated among the various colleges and universities. The libraries could not solve the problem of duplicate academic programs by restricting acquisitions in any field of study offered by parent institutions. Reducing courses and program replication lie within the purview of others, the parent institutions and the Commission.

To assess duplication of library materials, the Collection Development Committee analyzed the overlap of holdings supporting teacher education. This study found that 51 percent of the titles held by NAAL members were unique, that is, held by only one member. The rate of replication was only 2.6 volumes per title, a very low rate for a field with a high level of enrollment in schools throughout the state.[3] As a result, NAAL concluded that unnecessary duplication of resources was not a primary issue for statewide collection development. To help modify the expectations of the state leaders, this finding has been presented at appropriate opportunities and continues to be included in nearly every presentation made by NAAL.

The idea that NAAL would save money for its individual members haunted librarians on several fronts. First, some administrators thought that their libraries would no longer require substantial funding because sharing existing collections would somehow obviate the necessity of purchasing new materials. NAAL has had to stress that Network funds coordinate the activities that libraries can do together, but that local libraries and individual schools retain the responsibility for providing resources and services to their primary clientele. Second, the level of state revenue in Alabama is marked by wide fluctuations from year to year, and state law prohibits deficit spending. In tight years, the library budget, especially the materials budget, has been an easy target for university administrators forced to reduce expenditures. Some library directors have had their materials budget reduced or eliminated before the fiscal year could begin. Finally, some administrators thought that NAAL funding would replace institutional funding.

In NAAL's first year, one administrator cut the library budget by the amount received from NAAL. A "Maintenance of Effort Policy" was immediately adopted stating that eligibility for NAAL funding will be lost if library expenditures fall below those of the previous year. A procedure was also established for obtaining a waiver from the policy and provides a means to negotiate restoration of local funding in return for continued NAAL support.

An important test of the policy occurred in the 1990-91 fiscal year when the state experienced one of its not infrequent cycles in which revenues fail to meet allocations. All state budgets were reduced by a process known in Alabama as "proration." Proration typically occurs in an election year because the legislature appropriates more money than state revenue sources will generate. The legislative session in which the governor and legislators generously allocate substantial funding increases is convened before general statewide election. After the election, the negative consequences of shortfall in revenue must be addressed. Unexpected economic downturns also force proration on occasion. Almost without exception in 1990-91, university presidents protected library materials budgets after the 1990-91 proration. Necessary reductions were absorbed primarily by leaving vacated library positions unfilled.

Some success has been achieved in disabusing those holding the unrealistic expectations of the 1980s. To the chagrin of librarians, a new expectation is abroad. It is that all information is, or soon will be, available electronically and that it is somehow "free." The reality that only a tiny fraction of the world's information is available electronically is not reported in glowing reports about virtual or electronic libraries. Librarians find themselves vigorously defending expenditures for books and serials. However, they often leave those arguments feeling that the skeptics remain unconvinced. NAAL's program for collection development, which funds the acquisition of books, has been questioned as a waste of state resources. It has been suggested that NAAL should support only "high technology" projects because Alabama libraries can borrow anything they need from libraries out-of-state or obtain it electronically.

The library profession may be somewhat to blame for this unrealistic picture. Glowing reports about successful high tech library projects, "free" access to information via the Internet, and services soon to be available through the National Education and Research Network appear regularly in the library and higher education literature. Although many people embracing the high tech future have little or no personal experience with finding and retrieving information by electronic means, they seem convinced that libraries could be replaced today by a personal computer, a telephone line, and a modem.

IMPLEMENTING THE COOPERATIVE
COLLECTION DEVELOPMENT PROGRAM

Members of NAAL envisioned a complete online database of the holdings of its member libraries for the academic institutions supporting graduate education in Alabama. This "Alabama Research Collection" would serve as a powerful tool in providing bibliographic access to statewide library resources and would greatly facilitate access to those materials by identifying what was available. Further, it would serve as a firm foundation on which future NAAL programs could be built, including cooperative collection development.

NAAL's initial efforts focused on obtaining membership in OCLC through the Southeastern Library Network, Inc. (SOLINET) for each institution. Each NAAL member institution joined SOLINET at its own expense and agreed to add records of all of its newly-acquired materials to OCLC. NAAL committed to assisting each library in converting the card catalog records of existing holdings into machine-readable form through OCLC.

Consequently, NAAL's first program priority became retrospective conversion. A goal was set to add all catalog records for circulating print materials into OCLC within five years. NAAL allocated the majority of its funding to this Statewide Retrospective Conversion Program. To ensure success for retrospective conversion, no money was allocated to other programs, including collection development, in the early years.

In this manner, NAAL began to realize its "Alabama Research Collection," defined as the collective holdings of all the libraries of its academic members. While individual collections could not be rated "research level," the aggregate holdings would form a research level collection within the state. When all records for books and serials had been added to OCLC, any librarian would have bibliographic access to the holdings of all NAAL members.

In concept, this statewide online database representing the Alabama Research Collection would be the foundation for collection development and resource sharing. A cooperative Collection Development Program would identify deficiencies in statewide holdings and fund acquisitions to correct them. Further, a Resource Sharing Program would make the total library resources available to every student, faculty member, or other researcher engaged in graduate education or research through enhanced interlibrary loan services.

As noted earlier, *Cooperative Resource Sharing* had identified serious deficiencies in the collections of all the NAAL members. It was highly unlikely that the state's financial resources would improve dramatically to provide sufficient funds for any or all of Alabama's universities to develop collections that would adequately support their curricula and research. However, by working collaboratively to correct deficiencies in the *statewide* library resources, NAAL might develop a research-level collection for Alabama. To achieve this goal, the Network began to establish written policies and procedures that would define statewide cooperative collection development even though funds had not been provided to coordinate it.

Appointments to the initial Collection Development Committee included library directors and librarians responsible for some aspect of collection development. Alabama's chronic understaffing problems were evident, in this instance, by the inability of most libraries to consolidate collection development functions into one position. Functions normally identified with collection development resided in many positions: those of reference librarian, bibliographer, acquisitions librarian, and director. Only one library used the title, collection development librarian. In the remaining institutions no individual was assigned oversight for long-term collection planning and management. Several institutions still relied almost exclusively on teaching faculty for acquisitions decisions. The majority of librarians lacked training in activities commonly identified with collection development, especially in the areas of evaluation and policy development.

One of the first tasks of the Collection Development Committee was to work with the staff of ACHE to develop a library assessment component for the Commission's review of new academic program proposals. *Cooperative Library Resource Sharing* had noted a problem in the evaluation and approval of proposed new programs of instruction. While new programs had to be approved by ACHE, institutions were not required to consider the adequacy of library resources when seeking approval. ACHE had the necessary authority, which it did not exercise at that time, to require funding for needed library resources as a condition of approval. Ideally, this money would be provided by an increase in the library budget rather than by a mere reallocation of existing library funds. The latter would simply accommodate a new program at the expense of existing programs. Thus, the report recommended that ACHE work with the network to:

> develop a reasonable mechanism for reviewing library collection adequacy as part of the process of review and approval of new academic programs. This mechanism would ensure that collections adequate to support these programs are in place or will be funded within a minimum of five years from the program's approval.[4]

ACHE accepted this recommendation and agreed to require a library assessment report with any new program proposal submitted for its review. NAAL agreed to develop the assessment methodology for the library report. Both ACHE and NAAL needed a standardized methodology that could be applied consistently to most academic programs. Also, the amount of work required to implement the assessment would have to be acceptable to the institutions.

Paul Mosher, then at Stanford University and a recognized expert in cooperative collection development, served as consultant to NAAL for this project. He met with the Collection Development Committee to discuss methodology and provided valuable advice for the development of a collection assessment manual. Mosher's involvement was especially helpful in identifying activities that constitute collection development, evaluation methodologies, and training content. His ability to draw on the emerging RLG Conspectus and his consultancies in other states provided NAAL with valuable insight into national trends in cooperative collection development.

Published in 1985, the *NAAL Collection Assessment Manual*,[5] derived from existing collection assessment methodologies, especially the emerging RLG Conspectus. Workshops prepared librarians to evaluate collections for new programs and write the report required by ACHE. NAAL librarians in their first use of the methodology proved that it could be applied with relative consistency, that the amount of work required was acceptable, and that the resulting report was sufficient to guide planning for collection development. The *Manual* and its guidelines continue to be used with only minor modifications, which attests to the thoroughness of the Committee.

Its work on the *Manual* finished, the Committee turned its attention to the Network's responsibility to coordinate a statewide cooperative collection development program. The organic recommendation from *Cooperative Library Resource Sharing* was concise yet not prescriptive:

> [I]nitiate a statewide series of coordinated academic library collection analyses to identify collection strengths and weaknesses of each academic library....Eliminate existing quantitative and qualitative collection deficiencies....Develop guidelines for a statewide academic library shared collection development policy and procedures.[6]

Because the methodology developed for ACHE was working, it seemed appropriate to use it for NAAL's program. This offered the advantage of not requiring institutions to support multiple assessment methodologies and report formats.

An important debate in the early discussions of policy issues centered on how NAAL would identify and select subject areas that would receive NAAL funding. Committee members briefly considered selecting a few subjects, no more than five, that were important to the state's economic development. NAAL funds would concentrate on acquisitions to develop these collections to RLG

Research Level 4. When adequacy was achieved, new subjects would be chosen. An institution housing a "NAAL collection" would need to assure a high level of ongoing support or the adequacy of the collection would erode quickly once NAAL funding ended. The "select a few" approach elicited one of NAAL's icons, that it would create "spires of excellence on a swamp of mediocrity." Fred Heath, then at the University of North Alabama, used this phrase to argue against "select a few." It had such vivid impact that the Committee abandoned the concept almost immediately. This approach also violated an important principle of cooperation that all participants must benefit. Members without academic programs in areas selected to receive NAAL support would have found it difficult to gauge a tangible benefit.

NAAL eventually agreed that for all members to benefit from cooperation, some collection enhancement activities would have to be supported in each institution. Each institution was charged with identifying an area or areas in which it could contribute to statewide resources if supplemental funding were provided to correct deficiencies. Each member would receive funding for adding materials to its local collection that corrected deficiencies in the statewide holdings. Without knowledge of how much funding would ultimately be available, the Committee then began to develop an allocation formula that would equitably distribute funding to the members.

Funding

To distribute funds for its first program, Statewide Retrospective Conversion, NAAL had used a formula based on the number of records each institution needed to convert to machine-readable format. In the first year, each institution was awarded $11,000 to insure that there would be sufficient funds to initiate retrospective conversion at each library. After base payments were allocated, funds remaining in the "recon" line were awarded. Each institution received the same percent of the remaining funds that its number of records represented in the total number of records to be converted. The base was reduced by half each year and after four years was dropped from the formula. The "recon" formula, relying on volumes held, worked well. Because each member committed to adding records for its current acquisitions, the number of "recon" records to be added to OCLC was finite. The percentages used for calculating grants did not change, and this made each institution's funding predictable and stable from year to year.

NAAL members agreed that the "recon" formula would not be appropriate for collection development because it rewarded only historical collection size. Using such a basis would handicap the state's newer institutions because they had smaller collections. They reported intensive use of their collections including a high volume of lending to other libraries. It would also ignore serials holdings, an important component of the statewide resources. Also, appropriate factors for a collection development formula needed to be identified that would provide some incentive for the institutions to increase their own funding for library materials. Factors considered, but discarded, included number of graduate students, number of graduate programs, number of faculty, library expenditures as a percent of institutional expenditures, and number of interlibrary loans. After much discussion, NAAL adopted a formula based on number of volumes added annually and annual expenditures for library materials. Each factor received an equal weight. In the first year, the formula included a base amount to assist the institutions in the transition from the "recon" formula. With the base, no institution received less than it had received under the old formula. The base was reduced by half each succeeding year and was eliminated in four years. A stipulation was also added that NAAL funding would not exceed 25 percent of the institution's expenditures for library materials. This percent declined over four years to 15 percent (see Table 1).

All discussions from which the formula evolved occurred without consideration of actual dollars available. Only after agreement was reached on the underlying principles and the factors in the formula were hypothetical numbers calculated to estimate actual funding outcome. The applied formula correlates closely to measures of size such as number of students, number of graduate students, number of faculty, and library expenditures. Accordingly, larger institutions receive larger grants from NAAL but in turn contribute a greater proportion of materials to the state's total library resources and serve a greater number of students and faculty.

Table 1.   Statewide Collection Development Formula

The Statewide Collection Development Formula will:

1. allocate to each institution a base amount of $11,000 in FY90 which will be reduced by half each year and omitted in FY94;

2. use the number of volumes added annually by each institution expressed as a percentage of the total added for all institutions;

3. use the annual expenditures for library materials of each institution expressed as a percentage of the total expended by all institutions:

$$V/TV + E/TE = P$$

V = Volumes added annually by an institution;
TV = Total Volumes added annually by all institutions;
E = annual Expenditures for library materials by an institution;
TE = annual Total Expenditures for library materials by all institutions;
P = Percentage allocated to an institution; *and*

4. allocate an amount of NAAL funds that does not exceed 25 percent of the institution's expenditures for library materials in FY90, 20 percent in FY91, 17.5 percent in FY92, and 15 percent in FY93 and thereafter.

Training

In 1984, the number of volumes added annually by NAAL members ranged from 1,100 to 56,000. Few libraries had defined collection development as a separate function, and only one library maintained a separate collection development librarian position. As noted earlier, a variety of librarians performed collection development tasks as a part of their total responsibilities. A few institutions largely abdicated materials selection decisions to teaching faculty. Collection development as a planned, integrated responsibility for long term collection management hardly existed.

NAAL introduced the *Collection Assessment Manual* through a statewide workshop for librarians who would be involved in assessing collection support for new programs. These were usually the same individuals who would work with NAAL on the Collection Development Program. The *Manual* began by defining collection development and stressing the planning activities needed for the collection assessment accompanying new program proposals.[7] This first workshop introduced collection-centered assessment methodologies, including list-checking and citation analysis, and reviewed the expectations for a collection assessment report if a consultant were to assist in developing a new program. Reporting and interpreting quantifiable data were also covered. The methodology used for the RLG Conspectus and the then-available RLG subject worksheets were reviewed. A representative of the Alabama Commission on Higher Education described the final report format for new program proposals submitted to the Commission for review.

Librarians gained some confidence in their ability to complete assessments and to prepare new program proposal reports. The preferred methodology quickly became list-checking, using a sample if the list were long. Holdings on a standard list could be checked quickly and cheaply using student assistants, and the results appeared to give an irrefutable score of adequacy. Unfortunately, lists are dated by the time they are published. Many standard lists were not suitable for graduate-level study and merely provided an indication of the foundation on which the graduate resources could be built. Any title-by-title review usually elicited comments about newer or better publications more suited to the proposed curriculum.

Some librarians encountered hostility when an assessment determined that library resources could not support adequately the proposed curriculum. Estimates of the funds needed to initiate new subscriptions for essential serial subscriptions and backfiles along with estimates for an annual budget were often met with disbelief. In the worst of cases, the report prepared by the library was replaced in the proposal submitted to ACHE with a summary that reported adequacy where none existed. Teaching faculty and administrators wanted approval of their proposed programs and feared a "negative" library assessment would prevent approval. The Alabama Commission on Higher Education took a positive stance, noting that a low level of collection adequacy, by itself, would not prevent approval. However, it did note that approval would be dependent on a five-year plan to achieve adequacy. Even with this flexibility, librarians felt pressured to report findings of adequacy or to reduce the expenditures recommended to achieve adequacy.

Many librarians faced with challenging teaching faculty or administrators and upholding their findings indicated they needed a stronger foundation in collection development and assessment. In-state workshops, conducted by existing staff, had not provided sufficient expertise to defend a finding of inadequacy. To broaden the knowledge and skills of librarians, NAAL initiated a continuing education grant program. Each institution received an annual grant of $500 to assist with registration fees and travel expenses for its staff to attend a national or regional library training program. These grants were used to send staff to programs such as the ALCTS regional Seminars on Collection Management, ALA preconferences focusing on collections, or North American Serials Interest Group meetings. Participating in national activities, learning about successful programs in other libraries, and discovering how worrisome problems had been solved elsewhere helped build the expertise and confidence of Alabama's collection development librarians. This growing expertise forged a statewide corps of knowledgeable colleagues. Across the state, the quality of the assessments and the reports improved. From time to time, pressure may be brought to bear within an institution to revise an assessment detailing inadequate library resources for a proposed curriculum, but librarians can now more capably defend their data and findings.

The Alabama Commission on Higher Education has continued its flexibility by allowing institutions the five-year period in which to strengthen library resources for new programs. No penalties are imposed requiring an institution to allocate funds for new programs and, in practi ce, library budgets usually have not increased to support adequately new offerings. Despite the fact that acquisitions for new programs are sometimes still made (at the expense of existing programs, some libraries have obtained additional funding to address identified collection deficiencies. Even with this negative aspect of institutional funding practice, the policy requiring a library assessment for new program approval has been successful in improving the quality of resources available statewide and in providing a healthy focus on the need for stronger library support for academic programs. In many instances, too, local library materials budgets increased, though admittedly not enough,

Over time, most NAAL libraries have consolidated collection development responsibilities in one position. As the Collection Development Program continues to evolve, the individuals involved have accumulated remarkable expertise and are an asset to their individual institutions and to NAAL. It seems to meet NAAL's goal of supporting the library needs of graduate education in Alabama.

THE EVOLVING COOPERATIVE COLLECTION DEVELOPMENT PROGRAM

NAAL officially began funding its Collection Development Program in fiscal year 1985-86 when three members converted all of their catalog records to machine-readable format and asked to use their remaining "recon" funds for collection development. Three more members completed retrospective conversion the following year and asked to participate in collection development. Input of retrospective records had proceeded quickly. Consequently, the collection development formula completely replaced the retrospective conversion formula in fiscal year 1990-91, signaling the elevation of the cooperative collection development to NAAL's first priority. "Enlightened self-interest," a term borrowed from RLG, allowed each institution to choose the subject area or areas in which it would work on the statewide resources.

Early collection development proposals provided a test for NAAL's guidelines and brought to light questions and omissions not considered by the Committee. One such proposal requested NAAL assistance to improve a subject area in which a new doctoral-level program was being proposed. NAAL policies stipulated that NAAL funds could not be used for acquisitions supporting new programs. That was perceived to be the responsibility of the institutions. The school's representative argued that the library would be using the grant for the masters-level students it was already serving and that the proposal for the doctorate did not affect the need to strengthen the collection at that level. After some discussion, NAAL members agreed that Collection Development Program funds could not be used any area in which an institution proposes to add a new program or a new degree to an existing program. Further, NAAL funding would not be approved for five years after either was approved. Since then, several multi-year NAAL-funded collection development projects have been canceled because the institution suddenly proposed a new program or a new degree for an existing program. Twice, NAAL inadvertently enforced ACHE's requirements for library funding as a condition for approval of new programs. Both institutions involved sought to use NAAL grants in programs approved five years previously but for which substantive amounts of funding for acquisitions had been stipulated as a condition for approval. NAAL requested proof that ACHE's requirements had been met as a condition for the use of NAAL funds in the program. Neither institution had appropriated the required funds to the library. Both schools corrected that oversight so they would be eligible for NAAL assistance in the future.

"Enlightened self-interest" for selecting collection development subject areas did not lessen NAAL's emphasis on statewide goals. Several stipulations insured that the focus remained on statewide resources. The first of these, that all materials acquired with NAAL funds be made freely available to all other NAAL members, complemented the consortium's Resource Sharing Program guidelines for interlibrary loans. Under this program, all NAAL members lend their materials to all other members on the same basis that they lend those materials to their own users. No fees are charged to library users or between NAAL members. NAAL pays part of the interlibrary loans costs using a formula that funds net lenders first and then pays each member for both lending and borrowing activity. Photocopies are sent via telefacsimile; all other materials are sent via ground-based courier (UPS). Over time, effective document delivery has become an important supplement to the Collection Development Program. Participants agreeing to cooperate in collection development are less likely to object to the coordination of acquisitions if materials can be obtained quickly. Within NAAL, the average turnaround time for receipt of a requested item is less than five days. Most items are received by the borrowing library within two days after the request is placed. Because of this, most users are not unduly inconvenienced by the necessity of having materials they require retrieved from another location.

Enlightened Self-Interest

NAAL adopted the concept of enlightened self-interest in the belief that each institution is the appropriate entity to identify its own needs.

Each school, charged with assessing its own library resources in the context of statewide resources, can best determine how it contributes to the statewide resources. Enlightened self-interest reinforces the belief that cooperative collection development, to be successful, must respond to local institution needs and priorities if support is to be sustained. In addition, it acknowledges institutional commitments already in place and builds on these, strengthening support for the statewide program.

NAAL has placed some restrictions on the selection of subjects: All projects must develop collections supporting an approved and viable graduate education program. "Approved" requires an institution to have each graduate or first professional degree program listed in the state's *Inventory of Academic Programs.*[8] "Viable" means graduate students had enrolled and the institutions had conferred graduate degrees in the program in each of the last three years.

Local campus priorities play a role in the selection of disciplines for NAAL funding. In a positive way, the selection can reflect campus-wide aspirations. For example, the University of Alabama expanded its stress on international studies. This action did not require new academic programs, and the library developed several complementary proposals to emphasize that expansion: The central research library concentrated on acquisitions in world literature, world theater, and world politics; the Law Library acquired materials in international law; and the Business Library focused on international business. The development plan of each proposal was more specific, concentrating on genres, countries, or political themes and acquiring works in the original language as well as translation.

Politics and priorities of individual faculty members can be a blessing or a bane. NAAL encourages librarians to involve teaching faculty in assessing collections and writing collection development plans. Many faculty are supportive and help insure that the development plan corresponds to the curriculum. Unfortunately some faculty have viewed NAAL grants as a source of funds to acquire materials supporting their own research, regardless of whether this was reflected by the curriculum. Proposals have been submitted as a result of faculty pressure, but not approved by NAAL, in which the development plan had no relationship to the assessment but rather supported a faculty member's personal research agenda.

Occasionally, NAAL has had to cope with the efforts of faculty to control expenditures after grants had been awarded. Library directors were advised in writing that all grant expenditures would have to be consistent with the proposal approved by NAAL and that all acquisitions decisions would have to be made by the librarian who served as project director. Fortunately, these incidents are uncommon and increasingly unlikely to occur as faculty become aware of the guidelines for the Collection Development Program.

Since 1985, over $3.7 million dollars have been awarded for this NAAL program. The largest expenditures have been in science and technology, 24 percent of the total, and the humanities, 22 percent of the total. Subjects funded in science and technology include engineering, food and animal science, medicine, and allied health. Most of these projects stressed access to new information in rapidly changing disciplines and concentrated on acquiring current publications. They demonstrated the historical inadequate library funding on local campuses necessary to acquire the current materials needed to support the curricula in science and technology. Acquisitions in the humanities, largely foreign literature, Southern literature, and some English and contemporary American literature, concentrated on retrospective materials to fill gaps created by years of under funding. In these disciplines, the importance of historical research is apparent, and institutions felt the need to reduce their dependence on interlibrary loan for core materials. Education and business projects each accounted for 15 percent of the total NAAL collection development grant expenditures. (see Figure 1).

Expenditure patterns for the overall program mask the diversity of NAAL institutions when these are examined in three categories: institutions that belong to the Association of Southeastern Research Libraries (ASERL), regional publicly-supported institutions, and privately-supported institutions. Marked differences in program emphases emerge in each category.

The three NAAL ASERL members support ambitious research agendas and offer a wide array of doctoral and first professional degree academic programs. Two of these institutions are also members of the Association of Research Libraries. In addition to main libraries with branch libraries for science and engineering, architecture, and veterinary medicine, these institutions support a map library, law

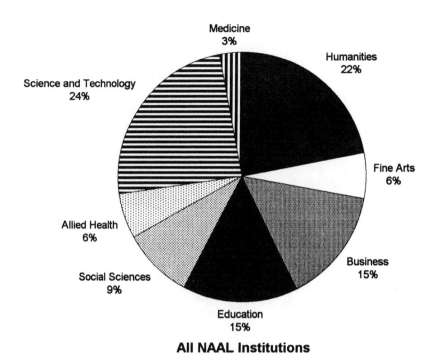

All NAAL Institutions

Figure 1. NAAL Funding for Collection Development, 1985-1994

library, and two medical libraries. Because the formula for distributing collection development grants correlates closely to institution size, 58 percent of the program funds from 1985 to 1994 were allocated to the three ASERL institutions. One-third of their NAAL grant expenditures were in the humanities and another one-third in science and technology. The next largest expenditure was in fine arts, 10 percent of the total. Although these institutions support the state's only doctoral degree programs in education, none used NAAL funds in this field. All have accredited business schools, but these expenditures were small, only 7 percent of the total, and all were for acquisitions in international business. They reflected a recent international emphasis by accrediting agencies and the state's growing awareness that economic development must occur within an international arena. (see Figure 2).

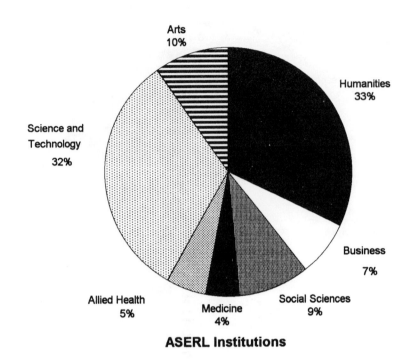

Arts
10%

Humanities
33%

Science and
Technology
32%

Business
7%

Allied Health
5%

Medicine
4%

Social Sciences
9%

ASERL Institutions

Figure 2.   NAAL Funding for Collection Development, 1985-1994

Eight of Alabama's eleven regional publicly-supported institutions were established primarily as normal schools. Although these institutions have added other programs in recent years, they continue to maintain large enrollments in teacher education. Three other regional publicly-supported institutions, created in the late 1960s or early 1970s, do not have a normal school tradition. Unfortunately, no special start-up funding was provided to establish libraries in these new schools, and, as a result, all lack historical materials. These eleven schools received 30 percent of the NAAL collection development grant funds from 1985 to 1994. Of the total grant expenditures to the regional publicly-supported institutions, 42 percent was used for education projects. This reflects the traditional teachers' college orientation and statewide demand for instruction in this field. The projects include several education specialties: music, history, English, social studies, learning disabilities, special education, multicultural education, and early childhood and elementary education. The initial proposals in education led to lengthy discussions about appropriate acquisitions in the discipline. NAAL did not want to encourage development of multiple unnecessarily replicative collections in education. Instead, the Collection Development Program sought to expand the quantity and the quality of information resources available within the state. Consequently, the institutions were encouraged to build strong foundations in the academic disciplines rather than to add duplicative pedagogical materials. For example, an institution choosing history education would be encouraged to acquire materials classified in history which support history education along with materials classified in history education. A proposal to acquire children's literature for an elementary education program resulted in a decision that creative works, even if intended for children, qualified as graduate level material eligible for purchase with NAAL funds. NAAL grants for acquisitions in education reflects the failure of library funding to keep pace with the expanding curriculum as the normal schools moved toward becoming broader-based universities. Acquisitions to support their new academic programs were made at the expense of adequate funding for education materials. Local library budgets have not expanded in concert with the curricula of those schools.

The second largest grant expenditure area for the regional publicly-supported institutions, 22 percent, was business. Assessments accompanying business collection development proposals most often found inadequate holdings in core materials. This demonstrated that almost all of the institutions had initiated this curriculum without providing adequate start-up or ongoing funding for business acquisitions.

The five privately-supported institutions are among NAAL's smallest members. Their NAAL grants represent only 11 percent of the collection development program funds from 1985 to 1994. Three of these are church-related institutions and have a strong liberal arts tradition. Another member, Tuskegee University, is a privately-supported, traditionally black institution whose mission is to provide scientific, technical, and professional education for its students. The remaining privately-supported institution, the U.S. Sports Academy,

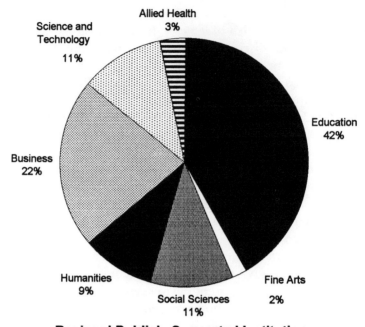

Regional Publicly-Supported Institutions

Figure 3.   NAAL Funding for Collection Development, 1985-1994

offers only graduate education in sports-related fields such as sports medicine, training, and management. Grant expenditures by the private institutions collectively are more diverse than those for the other two categories of NAAL members. Collection assessments for the three church-related schools indicated they supported adequately their traditional liberal arts curricula. However, these institutions shared with the regional publicly-supported institutions a trend toward more career-oriented offerings. Again, library funding had not increased to support adequately the acquisitions needed for these new programs, and assessments demonstrated significant gaps in core materials. Not surprisingly, the largest expenditures for the privately-supported schools were in business, 28 percent of the total. The second largest category of expenditures, 27 percent in science and technology, included only the grants to Tuskegee University. These

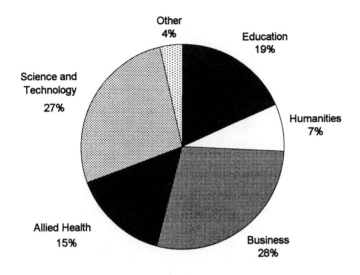

Private Institutions

Figure 4. NAAL Funding for Collection Development, 1985-1994

grants were used in two traditional programs at Tuskegee: food science and animal science. Education, 19 percent, and allied health, 15 percent, also reflected a growing number of professional programs in the private institutions.

Much discussion about church and state separation was precipitated by a proposal by Spring Hill College, a Jesuit institution, to acquire materials for late Patristic and Middle Ages studies. The proposal was clearly non-denominational, but NAAL felt it needed to avoid even the appearance that state funds were supporting the acquisition of sectarian materials. The proposal was approved, and NAAL added a new guideline to its policy stating that funds could not be expended to acquire library materials for sectarian instruction or worship, primarily in connection with any part of a program of a school or department of divinity. Spring Hill College is also using NAAL funds to develop its business ethics collection, complementing an already strong collection in ethics, and is becoming a state resource center for research in this field.

Projects in the Same Disciplines

An examination of individual grants reveals that several institutions have collection development projects that include the same disciplines. For example, in fiscal year 1993-94, six projects are developing collections in business. Two institutions are strengthening their collections of foreign literature. Since 1985, there have been thirty-four projects in education. Surprisingly, even with the schools selecting subject areas for development, the collection development plans for acquisitions reveal little duplication in the same discipline. For example, the business projects are in economics, maritime industries, and international business. The three international business plans emphasize different aspects: Russia and Eastern Europe, the Pacific Rim, and the European Common Market. The thirty-four development plans in education are all different and generally complement each other.

Awarding grants for several projects in the same discipline raised the issue of how best to attain a statewide research level collection in the discipline. Without careful coordination of acquisitions on an item-by-item basis, unintentional duplication of materials might preclude the acquisition of a greater number of titles in the field. Would lack of coordination among projects in the same discipline prevent NAAL from accomplishing its goal of a statewide research collection?

The RLG Conspectus methodology notes that several institutions with collections rated at one level may collectively rate a higher level. Thus, several NAAL institutions with subject collections rated Instructional Support Level (3) might collectively achieve Research Level (4). To test this assumption, the holdings of NAAL members in education were checked against several standardized lists. Each education project reports the results of checking holdings of education titles listed in *Books for College Libraries* (3rd ed. *BCL3*), a selective list of titles recommended in *Choice* for undergraduate education which includes many titles also recommended for graduate education. Institutions that have checked the entire education section in *BCL3* reported holding from 42 percent to 70 percent of the titles listed. A check of the statewide database found at least one copy of all but three of the 1,087 education titles in *BCL3*, or 99.7 percent of the total. Such substantial holdings demonstrated that NAAL libraries have a strong core of literature supporting their education programs.

Checking titles from *Books for College Libraries* assesses only historical materials. To judge holdings of current acquisitions, a sample of 119 of 708 titles classified in education and listed in *American Book Publishing Record* (1989) and a sample of 132 of 787 titles listed in *American Book Publishing Record* (1990) were checked for statewide holdings. In July 1993, 500 occurrences of the 119 titles in the 1989 sample revealed a duplication rate of 4.2 volumes per title. Collectively, the NAAL libraries held 90.8 percent of the sample titles. There were 437 occurrences of the 132 titles in the 1990 sample, also checked in July 1993. The duplication rate was 3.31 volumes per title; the libraries held 82.6 percent of the titles. The *American Book Publishing Record*, a list of books published in the subject annually, is not selective. However, the strong holdings found for these samples are more representative of current collecting intensity in education than checking a standardized list. Collecting intensity attempts to gauge overall coverage in acquisitions for the field.

None of the standardized lists furnish good measures for federal publications or for materials held in microform. However, after Auburn University added records for its federal publications into its local catalog, NAAL funded the uploading of tapes of these records into OCLC to facilitate bibliographic access and resource sharing. In addition, several major microform sets in education are included in the microforms for which NAAL has set holding symbols in OCLC. Access to these materials improved markedly statewide.

The libraries also checked their current subscriptions against titles indexed in *Education Index*. All but two titles were held by at least one NAAL member. The data resulting from checking these lists indicate that Alabama is close to attaining a statewide research level collection in education. This has been achieved without designating collecting responsibilities or restricting development grants to only one project in a discipline. Further, the duplication rate of 4.2 volumes per titles found for the 1989 sample from *American Book Publishing Record* is not deemed excessive. This is not a high rate of duplication for a field such as education which has very high student enrollment and in which a large number of degrees are conferred.

NAAL's willingness to approve multiple projects in one discipline grew out of early concerns that the first grant for a subject would assign exclusive rights for NAAL funds for that subject to the first applicant. The NAAL Collection Development Committee was equally concerned that without assigned subject responsibility, enlightened self-interest would result in highly duplicative collections because of the existence of duplicative programs. In practice, the NAAL members have shown remarkable adherence to the expectation that NAAL will reduce unnecessary duplication. Institutions make every effort to assure that their individual development plans expand the total information resources available in the state. List-checking for statewide holdings in education seems to demonstrate that several Level 3 collections can attain Level 4 if their holdings are considered collectively. Even with thirty-four projects in education, the level of duplication for current acquisitions, judging from the samples from *American Book Publishing Records*, is low. NAAL's policy establishing acquisition priorities for nonduplicative monographs and unique serial backfiles before the purchase of duplicative monographs and serial backfiles facilitates diversity in collections. Consequently, closer coordination of acquisitions or restrictions on the number of projects approved for a discipline does not seem warranted. Therefore, it appears unlikely that NAAL will replace enlightened self-interest as the basis for identifying disciplines requiring NAAL assistance.

Serials

When NAAL was first established, an annual appropriation from the Alabama Legislature was not assured. Without stable long-term funding, NAAL hesitated to use its funds to enter new subscriptions for serials which would be canceled if NAAL funding were lost. Collection reviews nearly always demonstrate the need for additional subscriptions, but these must be acquired with local funds. With a few restrictions, serial backfiles may be acquired with NAAL funds. First, institutions must have a current subscription to any title for which backfiles will be obtained. Second, institutions must consider the availability of backfiles within the state. NAAL funds may be used only to acquire those that are not duplicative; or, if duplicative, relieve an interlibrary loan burden. After reviewing research into the use of serial literature, NAAL also asked the institutions to avoid acquiring backfiles older than five years unless they can be shown to be unique to the state and essential for an academic program. Most retrospective needs for serials have been met through interlibrary loan. Finally, NAAL does not approve funding to replace lost and missing serials. Replacement is a local institution obligation.

Constraints on funding for local acquisitions have forced several consortium members to reduce expenditures for serials and make major cuts in current subscriptions. In response to this phenomenon, the Collection Development Committee has established a subcommittee to address an appropriate role for NAAL in statewide coordination of serials collections. Issues under study include coordination of serials cuts to insure at least one subscription remains in the state, the use of online full-text databases in lieu of print subscriptions, and an appropriate future role for NAAL in funding serials.

Reference Materials and Business Services

NAAL policy affirms that it is an institutional responsibility to provide the bibliographic and other reference tools that enable users to access knowledge in a field. Business service publications, which are both serial and reference by nature, are also considered the acquisitions responsibility of the schools. Most libraries are reluctant to lend reference and business service items because of their heavy in-house use. Because all materials purchased with NAAL funds or their surrogates must be lent via interlibrary loan to any other NAAL members, these two types of materials cannot be purchased as part of a NAAL collection development grant. Many bibliographic tools and business services are now available in CD-ROM format but cannot be bought with NAAL funds for the reasons noted above.

Non-Print and Microforms

NAAL's policy for acquiring nonprint material is less defined. Several early proposals requested the acquisition of materials such as videotapes, slides, and microform reproductions of print materials. Most nonprint material is excluded because NAAL funds cannot be used to acquire classroom instructional materials or materials that cannot be shared easily through interlibrary loan. As the CD-ROM becomes an acceptable format for publication of materials other than those intended primarily for reference and as libraries agree to lend the discs, NAAL may have to reconsider whether its funds can be used for these media.

NAAL members hold substantial microform collections. Formulating an effective policy for their acquisition has been difficult. However, microform frequently may be the only format in which needed research materials are available. Bibliographic control is inadequate, and user access to individual titles in sets is difficult. Researchers often resist using the format, regardless of how badly the information may be desired. Within NAAL, microforms are freely shared by duplicating microfiche, lending microfilm, or printing copies from either format. Even with this generous sharing policy, the use of NAAL funds to acquire microforms is discouraged, but not altogether prohibited. Proposals must defend the need for the content of the microform, detail the availability of machine-readable cataloging records, provide a plan to add these records to OCLC, and describe bibliographic tools that other libraries can acquire to make full use of the microforms.

NAAL publishes a union list of microform sets to improve bibliographic control and increase user access. Members contribute information about holdings of the sets, and the union list is distributed as a WordPerfect or ASCII file. The union list includes information about indexes and other finding tools, as well, and librarians are encouraged to acquire copies of these or to call holding libraries for reference assistance. Further, the consortium funds the addition of set holding symbols on OCLC for cataloged sets held in their entirely by its members. This has proven to be a very inexpensive way to increase access. NAAL has added its members holding symbols to 300,000 records representing titles held in thirty-four major microform sets for which records are available from OCLC. The libraries add the machine-readable records to their local public access catalogs, increasing access in the local academic library. Unfortunately, OCLC has denied a request by NAAL members to add the microform records to the state's union catalog, distributed in CD-ROM format to the state's public libraries, to increase access to the materials to Alabamians outside the academic community. In fiscal year 1993-94, a federal grant to NAAL will enable eight NOTIS libraries to create an interactive online network via the Internet. Through these linked systems, users will have access to the microform records loaded into local library catalogs. This will enhance knowledge about these resources and should increase their use.

Research (Level 4) Materials

The primary emphasis of the Collection Development Program has been to strengthen collections supporting graduate education, generally described as RLG Conspectus Level 3 or Instructional Support Level. Because NAAL's mission includes strengthening collections supporting research, it inaugurated a Research Support grants program in fiscal year 1989-90. Materials purchased with Research Support grants were used to strengthen collections supporting statewide research purposes. Research Support grants enabled an institution to acquire expensive items which lay beyond its own financial capability. Only items unique to the state could be purchased using a Research Support grant.

To implement acquisitions at the research level, NAAL set aside ten percent of the funds allocated for the Collection Development Program and instituted a competitive grant process. In the first year, proposals were approved for Black studies, English literature, music, and part of the U.S. patents backfiles. In the second year, materials in aerospace history, biomedical engineering, forensic science, English literature, geriatrics, and the remaining U.S. patents backfiles, were acquired. Several of these projects were to buy large microform sets. The acquisition of large microform sets without machine-readable records which could be added to OCLC caused concern about how easily the individual items could be identified and located by researchers throughout the state. However, the sets did contain needed research materials which were unattainable in print format and were approved for acquisition. Tuskegee University acquired the then-available units of *Black Literature* (Chadwyck-Healey), *Black Biographical Dictionaries* (Chadwyck-Healey),

selected units from *Black Journals* (University Publications of
America), and the *Schomburg Clipping File*. The University of
Alabama at Birmingham received grants for two years to complete
acquisition of *The Eighteenth Century* (Research Publications).
Auburn University acquired the U.S. Patents backfiles over two
years.

In fiscal year 1991-92, the reduction in NAAL's appropriation did
not provide sufficient funds to justify the ten percent set aside, and
the program was suspended. In fiscal year 1993-94, NAAL revised
its guidelines to allow Research Support projects as part of the regular
allocation for collection development, which had formerly been
restricted to Instructional Support. New Research Support projects
must meet the NAAL guidelines for Research Support grants but
do not have to be linked to an approved and viable graduate program
at the institution.

THE FUTURE IS NOT WHAT IT USED TO BE

NAAL's collection development goal is likely to remain the same in
the near future: to improve statewide information resources in
support of graduate education and research. Like other research
institutions, individual NAAL members will continue to rely on the
availability of external information resources. The envisioned
"Alabama Research Collection" will not be entirely self-sufficient.
However, by working together, Alabama academic institutions can
meet a growing number of their users' information needs from their
local resources or the collective resources of the NAAL members.
Several developments are converging to change the way all libraries
function individually as well as within consortia. Consequently, the
NAAL approach to collection development coordination may
change.

Reduced funding from the state is the first development likely to
force substantial change in the Collection Development Program.
Sufficient external funding to insure that NAAL collection
development grants could strengthen the local as well as the statewide
collection has been critical to the success of the Collection
Development Program. Evaluations of collections following two or

three years of NAAL assistance demonstrated tangible improvement. Percentages of titles found on standardized lists routinely began to exceed 50 percent and often approached 70 percent.[9] NAAL libraries increased their percentage of interlibrary loans filled from in-state resources from 32 percent in 1985 to 61 percent in 1990. With the completion of the Statewide Retrospective Conversion Program and the addition of new materials made possible by the Collection Development Program, NAAL libraries as a group became net lenders to the collective OCLC libraries in every other state.[10] External funding for cooperative collection development helped build a greater degree of self-sufficiency for the collective Alabama academic libraries.

In its first year, the Collection Development Program distributed $43,000 to three institutions. By fiscal year 1989-90, a peak of nearly $850,000 was distributed in collection development grants. Unfortunately, in fiscal year 1990-91, Alabama experienced one of its cyclical "revenues fail to meet projections," and all state appropriations were reduced. Subsequent reductions in state appropriations to enable the state to operate within its revenue resulted in a 41 percent reduction in the NAAL appropriation by fiscal year fiscal year 1993-94. Since fiscal year 1990-91, funding for the Collection Development Program has declined annually having an expenditure potential of only $252,000 in fiscal year 1993-94. Given an average current cost of about $46 for a monograph, grants of only a few thousand dollars cannot support a sufficient level of acquisitions to achieve a measurable difference in the quality of a collection. Smaller institutions are beginning to question the amount of work required to develop a proposal and administer a grant in relation to the amount of funding received.

Another development pressing NAAL to change is the evolution of technology supporting scholarly communication. The Collection Development Program guidelines were developed in an environment saturated by print. Information is available in an electronic format; in many cases, it is not available in print. It is increasingly less essential for the information *package*, regardless of format, to be located physically in the library. Paying a fee for online remote database accessibility may sometimes be a less expensive alternative to owning the information. The widespread availability of Internet or other telecommunications networks allows libraries to offer access to materials which cannot be owned by sharing the expense of maintaining online databases, especially full-text databases. Also, it may be unreasonable for NAAL to expect its members to abide by the Maintenance of Effort Policy, which requires sustained support for acquiring primarily print materials, if expenditures in automation and telecommunications can achieve a greater level of service for the library user.

An important development affecting the future of the Cooperative Collection Development Program is the implementation of NAAL's Electronic Access Program. This program grew out of efforts begun in 1985 to plan a statewide interactive online network. In 1993, NAAL received HEA Title II-A funding to link eight NOTIS systems as Phase I in its statewide plan. Other phases will link other library systems into the network, provide access to shared databases, and offer gateway services to remotely-installed databases. NAAL allocated funds for the first time to the Electronic Access Program in fiscal year 1993-94. The Network also adopted a policy allowing institutions to choose participation in the Electronic Access Program by using their Collection Development Program allocation for electronic access activities. Only one institution chose Electronic Access rather than Collection Development in the first year, but other institutions are interested in using the option in fiscal year 1994-95. The Electronic Access Program funds may be used to provide gateway and other electronic information services, share the cost of acquiring and loading online databases, and pay the licensing fees for access to databases installed by one of the NAAL institutions. By approving funding for these activities in lieu of funding the acquisition of traditional print materials, the Network recognized the increasing importance of providing information service regardless of information format.

The prospect of reduced funding, changing technology, and the implementation of the interactive online network will change in the Collection Development Program but not NAAL's charge to strengthen collections supporting graduate education and research. To prepare for a changed future, NAAL has begun to examine its charge and to consider its alternatives. Its members will bring to the process the same democratic deliberation that marked their early planning. Any program that replaces the current collection development program will surely continue to propel the academic libraries in Alabama toward improving their ability to meet the information needs of their users.

NOTES AND REFERENCES

1. *Cooperative Library Resource Sharing among Universities Supporting Graduate Study in Alabama* (Montgomery, AL: Alabama Commission on Higher Education, 1983). (ERIC Document Reproduction Service No. ED 224 497).
2. Sue O. Medina and William C. Highfill, "Effective Governance in a State Academic Network: The Experience of the Network of Alabama Academic Libraries," *Library Administration and Management* 6(Winter 1992): 15-20.
3. Fred Heath, "An Assessment of Education Holdings in Alabama Academic Libraries: A Collection Analysis Project," in *Cooperative Collection Development, Proceedings of the June 1991 ASCLA Multi-LINCS Preconference*, comp. Diane Macht Solomon, (Chicago: Association of Specialized and Cooperative Library Agencies, 1992), pp. 37-65.
4. Ibid., p. 47.
5. Network of Alabama Academic Libraries, *Collection Assessment Manual* (Montgomery, AL: The Network, 1985). (ERIC Document Reproduction Service No. ED 290 462).
6. Ibid., p. 47.
7. For NAAL, collection development includes the activities typically related to planning: establishing mission and policy statements, describing existing conditions, reviewing strengths and weaknesses, considering external and internal factors and trends, setting goals, developing strategies to meet goals, and evaluating success in meeting goals. It includes the traditional functions of selection, acquisition, assessment, gifts and exchange, conservation, preservation, and weeding.
8. *Inventory of Academic Programs* (Montgomery, AL: Alabama Commission on Higher Education, annual).
9. NAAL considers a standardized list as a surrogate user. The user should be able to find 50 percent of the items on the list held by the local library. Through interlibrary loan, the library should be able to obtain up to 60 percent of the list by using in-state resources and up to 85 percent from national resources.
10. NAAL compiles these interlibrary loan data from the *OCLC ILL Monthly Activity Reports*, year-to-date totals are provided annually in June.

RESOURCE SHARING IDEALS AND REALITIES:

THE CASE OF AUSTRALIA'S DISTRIBUTED NATIONAL COLLECTION

Margaret Henty

INTRODUCTION

Libraries throughout the world are acknowledging their increasing interdependence and the growing recognition that self-sufficiency is unattainable. Resource sharing has been written about at length in the library literature and is now becoming a reality for those who define the necessary mechanisms, costs, and rewards. In Australia, a national approach to resource sharing has been developed based on the idea that the country possesses a distributed national collection that can be developed collaboratively for the common good. This

Advances in Collection Development and Resource Management,
Volume 1, pages 139-152.
Copyright © 1995 by JAI Press Inc.
All rights of reproduction in any form reserved.
ISBN: 1-55938-213-9

concept has provided a focus for a wide range of cooperative activities that have gained support at all levels.

Australia is a large country about the size of the mainland United States. Its population is, for the most part, distributed around the coastline and heavily urbanized into ten or so main cities. The total population is about seventeen million, largely of British stock, but becoming increasingly ethnically diverse since World War II, initially through a wave of European migration, and more recently with arrivals from Asia. Culturally and economically, there has been a move to develop ties with our Asian neighbours within the past few years, changing the nation's traditional cultural and linguistic focus. A tightening economy has led to greater economic stringency and a more general acceptance of the notion of 'user pays'. Higher education is increasingly in demand, as the economy moves from its traditional reliance on agriculture and mineral resources to a sophisticated manufacturing base. Not only are more young people seeking higher education, but adult education has become more readily accepted.

Politically, Australia is a federation of six states and two territories, so there are three layers of government: federal, state, and local. Each government authority has its own funding mechanisms and its own priorities, making it difficult for public sector libraries, which form the majority, to coordinate their collections and services. There are three major Australian library associations set up to support their members and to coordinate cooperative programs. The Australian Council of Libraries and Information Services (ACLIS) is a cross sectoral association with over 600 members. Set up in 1988, it is supported by the National Library of Australia and includes most academic libraries, all state libraries, and a wide cross-section of public and special libraries. The Council of Australian State Libraries (CASL) represents the state and territorial libraries, which together house much of Australia's documentary heritage material. The Council of Australian University Librarians (CAUL) represents higher education libraries of which all but a few are funded through the federal Department of Employment, Education and Training.

Australian libraries are responding to the needs of a changing society by seeking new means and opportunities to improve services. As in libraries in other countries, not only are cultural and economic forces changing, but the world of information supply is itself changing. Technology has changed the ways by which information can be organized and delivered. Improvements in the ease of bibliographic access, largely as a result of technology, have brought increased demand for the documents themselves. Technological developments have provided the opportunity to link bibliographic access to sources of document supply, and electronic publishing is rapidly becoming a reality. More information is being produced each year, and costs, especially for serials, have proved difficult to contain. The condition of library collections is deteriorating, primarily due to the use of acid-based papers and other nonpermanent materials. The establishment of AARNet (the Australian Academic and Research Network) in 1991 has connected Australian academic institutions to the Internet, changing many of the ways in which libraries operate. The development of a 'distributed electronic collection' adds a new dimension to information supply, preservation needs, and issues of identification and bibliographic control.

Australian libraries, about 13,000 of them, vary widely in size and quality.[1] The largest group is composed of some 10,000 primary and secondary schools. There are about 1,400 public libraries, serving over six million registered users and more than 1,000 special libraries serving government departments, large and small business enterprises, and other specialist user groups. One special library of particular significance is the library of the Commonwealth Scientific and Industrial Research Organisation, CSIRO, the preeminent scientific and technological library in the country.

The largest libraries, however, are of two types, the libraries of higher education institutions on the one hand, and the National Library and six State Libraries on the other. These last two groups are estimated to hold collectively more than forty million volumes. The two largest collections in the country are held by the National Library of Australia, with about five million items, and the Library of the University of Sydney with over three million.

THE CONCEPT

In 1988, there was a meeting of more than 100 representatives of Australian libraries and library associations. Resolution AA1 of the

Australian Libraries Summit, as it is known, formalized the following
principles that a national collection be

1. an aggregation of all library collections in Australia whether
    in the public or private sector;
2. comprehensive in relation to Australia;
3. selective in relation to the rest of the world as present and
    future needs require; and
4. adequately recorded and readily accessible.

While the idea of a distributed national collection itself is not new,
its formalization provides the Australian library community with an
opportunity to look to the further development of local and regional
library services within a wider context. Libraries have always been to
some extent interdependent, and an ad hoc system of library
cooperation has existed for many years, enabling the functioning of,
for example, the interlibrary loans system. The concept of a distributed
national collection provides for the development of an infrastructure
of cooperative mechanisms and strategies that have the potential to
provide an overall strengthening of library services. There has never
been an agreement on precisely how formal a development is
postulated: it is generally recognized that the present loose system of
cooperation provides one end of a spectrum, while a formal cooperative
arrangement with designated collecting roles provides the other.

GATHERING SUPPORT

The Australian Libraries Summit of 1988 presented to the library
community the possibility of viewing the national collection as one.
There was support from a sufficient number of libraries to ensure
ongoing support for more formal development of this collection. In
the five years since then, that commitment to collaboration has
widened with support from government and other stakeholders. A
meeting of Australian academic librarians, together with other major
figures from the Australian library community including the National
Library, reaffirmed their mutual commitment to the distributed
national collection in March 1993.

Political support has gradually been generated at both federal and state levels. The Working Party established to review library provision in higher education libraries in 1990 specifically mentioned the desirability of developing the distributed national collection:

> On one matter there is no dispute. In the absence of a comprehensive central library, the national interest requires that the principal libraries in Australia be recognized as a single national resource, now described as the distributed national collection.[2]

Since that influential report, support has also come from other sources. The Report of the House of Representatives Standing Committee for Long Term Strategies, Australia as an Information Society: The Role of Libraries/Information Networks also accepted the concept.

> It would seem to the Committee that a solution to the problems of access, equity and funding, and a logical extension of the Australian Bibliographic Network is the concept of the Distributed National Collection. In a country with a small and dispersed population this would seem to be a necessary way to overcome problems of equity and access and the rapidly rising cost of materials. Modern technology should make materials held in widespread geographic locations increasingly accessible.[3]

Most recently, the concept appeared in the cultural policy put forth by the Australian Labor Party in the lead up to the 1993 federal election. However, to the surprise of librarians, the term was applied to a broader category of materials. Under the heading "Distributed national collection," the policy stated: "Our nation's cultural memory is stored in museums, galleries, libraries, archives and individual collections throughout Australia."[4] The Labor Party went on to win that election, and has made good its pledge to commit A$2 million over four years, although how much will come to libraries remains to be seen.

Other positive moves are evident from the interest shown by the Australian Vice-Chancellors' Committee, the committee of chief executive officers from Australia's universities. This group has come to recognize that it is responsible for most of the significant research collections within the country and has expressed interest in investigating mechanisms for future collaborative developments. The commitment of senior administrators to future developments is of

major significance, especially as it relates to the universities'
understandable reluctance to rationalize research programs.

PROGRESS TO DATE

In practice there are five aspects of the distributed national collection
that are receiving attention from Australian libraries: collections,
bibliographic control, preservation, access, and national coordination. Key roles have so far been taken by the Australian Council of
Libraries and Information Services (ACLIS) and the National
Library of Australia in establishing policies and mechanisms that
provide a basis for ongoing development. Other bodies committed
to the concept include the Council of Australian State Libraries and
the Council of Australian University Librarians.

COLLECTIONS

Collaborative collection development is hampered by a lack of
understanding of the existing strengths and collecting intentions of
other libraries, so there need to be mechanisms whereby this
information can be shared. Such mechanisms include the
establishment of a national conspectus database and encouragement
to provide collection development policies that can be made widely
known in a standardizsed form. Even without the assignment of
collecting responsibilities, a knowledge of what other libraries are
doing should assist in reducing duplication of collecting and in
maximizing individual titles available in the country. A survey carried
out late in 1992 by ACLIS showed high levels of support for the idea
of collecting agreements, although academic libraries acknowledged
that they would not be in a position to undertake collecting in areas
that did not correspond to the research and teaching needs of their
institutions. There was general agreement that libraries that take
responsibility for defined areas of collecting would not only acquire
materials, but would make their whereabouts known through a
nationally available bibliographic utility such as the national
bibliographic database and provide access to the collection for bona
fide researchers. The provision of materials for undergraduate

teaching would presumably remain the responsibility of the teaching institution so that national collecting responsibilities would be most likely restricted to more broadly ranging research materials, although improvements in bibliographic access are blurring whatever distinction there may have been between research and teaching collections.

So far there has been interest in collaborative collecting arrangements on a national basis in subject areas such as Latin American studies, Asian studies, and medicine. Examples can be seen in the handing over of South American materials by the National Library of Australia to La Trobe University and the agreement between the Northern Territory University and the National Library whereby the former has agreed to collect East Indonesian materials and the latter materials from other parts of Indonesia.

BIBLIOGRAPHIC CONTROL

The linking of libraries through the Australian Bibliographic Network (ABN) has enabled the development of a national bibliographic database (NBD) of holdings of individual titles to which libraries can refer when seeking to borrow materials for users. The Australian Bibliographic Network was established by the National Library in 1981 as a shared cataloging facility. Since then it has grown to be the most significant source of holdings data in the country and connects to an interlending module to expedite document supply. It hosts Ozline, a set of databases providing indexes to materials in the social sciences and humanities, the most significant being the Australian Public Affairs Information Service (APAIS). A module is currently being developed to accommodate Chinese, Japanese, and Korean records. The planned redevelopment of ABN to create a National Document and Information Service (NDIS) is being carried out jointly by the National Libraries of Australia and New Zealand. It will link bibliographic records with sources of documents by incorporating holdings records and by permitting access to full text either in digitized or in scanned form. Other features of the NDIS will include online access to the national conspectus databases of each country and an ability to incorporate index level entries.

The ongoing development of the national bibliographic database is one key element in the development of the distributed national collection. The major current contributors are the academic libraries with significant other holdings coming from public libraries, the National Library, and the state libraries. As the database grows, it incorporates more nonbook materials such as maps, music, manuscripts, pictorial items, or oral history collections, and as library catalogs are progressively converted to electronic form, more materials of historical interest are included. As at 31 August 1993, the records in the NBD included:[5]

Bibliographic file	=	9,991,555
Holdings statements	=	18,303,463
Authority file	=	1,284,879
Original cataloging	=	1,330,119

In order to improve the national bibliographic database, it will be necessary to extend its coverage and to extend the range of functions which it serves. Encouragement to add records to the database is made by a system of credits given for new catalog records added (at present US$10 per record). Holdings are added by participating libraries as their catalogs are converted to electronic form, for which there is also a financial incentive (US$0.72). Some of the larger libraries face a lengthy process in adding all their records to the national database, and in some cases, special one-off grants from the Federal Department of Employment, Education and Training have been obtained to mount holdings in the national interest.

PRESERVATION

There is a need for a nationally coordinated approach to the preservation of the Australian documentary record and to those non-Australian materials to which future access should be assured. Considerable work has been done by ACLIS in identifying materials at risk, and the creation of a National Preservation Office in the National Library will provide a future focus for cooperative activity. Activities underway at present include the establishment of a national newspaper plan to microform Australian newspapers, the establishment of standards for permanent paper and for aspects of preservation microfilming, and the support of preservation management training workshops in various countries in Asia and the Pacific.

Progress is being made to allow libraries to record preservation intention on the database. Other preservation related developments include a facility for the inclusion of the location of microfilm masters.

ACCESS

The key to the success of the distributed national collection is access. Activity in this area has been directed toward the improvement of ordering and supply mechanisms for materials needed at a distance and the introduction of reciprocal borrowing schemes, which have been successfully introduced in some regions. Prompt document supply is being assisted by technological developments that allow the ordering, scanning, and electronic transmission of documents. Much attention has been paid to the introduction of a national interlending code and the establishment of an agreed scale of charges.

The most important issue regarding access has been that of charging. Many librarians see libraries as a common good that should be available freely to all. Others argue that their library is there to meet the specific needs of their institutions (which provide their funding) and that they have no obligation to meet the needs of outsiders without due recognition of the costs involved. As library collecting is cut back and as libraries turn to notions of access rather than ownership, it is critical that the issue of financial responsibility be addressed and that net lenders not be expected to carry a burden that lies beyond their charter. ACLIS, to date, has done well to have introduced a scale of charges that have been widely accepted. The charges are below those set by the newly emerging commercial document suppliers, although the latter may have the edge in terms of prompt delivery. Some libraries have set up groups that supply free of charge on a reciprocal basis; about one half of interlibrary loan transactions take place without charge. These groups are usually based on common interest such as health, or they may be public libraries connected to a state library that accepts a responsibility to supply at no cost.

A second important issue regarding access is the introduction of communications technology that allows end-users to bypass the library and order documents directly. In Australia, this trend is becoming more apparent with recent decisions to extend access to the Australian Bibliographic Network to library users and not just to libraries as before. In addition, major databases, such as Current Contents, have recently become nationally available to academic libraries through AARNet, with links to document supply mechanisms.

NATIONAL COORDINATION

The primary advantage of a formalised distributed national collection concept has been the opportunity to focus on cooperative strategies at both regional and national levels to improve library services. To date, a major role has been taken by ACLIS which has done much to publicize the concept and to contribute to ongoing planning and policy development by, for example, conducting research on the distributed national collection, supporting the initial development of conspectus, and developing interlibrary lending codes and charges. The National Library has also had a key role, derived primarily from its statutory function as a national information provider. The National Library hosts the Australian Bibliographic Network and has set up the National Preservation Office. More recently it has announced the establishment of a special unit with responsibility for collection-related matters such as conspectus and other mechanisms for sharing knowledge about collections.

TOWARD FEDERATION 2001

Part of the definition of the distributed national collection refers to the need for it to be "comprehensive in relation to Australia." While this is relatively easy to envisage in terms of published materials, it is less clear what comprehensive means in terms of other materials such as ephemera, manuscripts, oral history records, and pictorial items.[6] There is no institution that has overall responsibility for collecting unpublished records (other than national and state archives for government records), and the scope for such collecting is open-ended. At the federal level, there are a number of institutions that collect systematically, such as the National Library, National Film and Sound Archive, Australian War Memorial, National Gallery of Australia, and the National Maritime Museum, to name but a few. At the State/Territory level there are more, including State libraries, higher education institutions, and public and special libraries. The aim of bringing all kinds of documentary material into the distributed national collection has been pursued through the establishment of cooperative programs designed to ensure the identification and preservation of the Australian documentary heritage. A conference, Towards Federation 2001: Linking Australians and Their Heritage, was held in Canberra in March 1992 and was attended by 140 invited participants, drawn from the nation's libraries, archives and other national collecting institutions and a range of other organisations concerned with publishing, collecting and preserving Australia's documentary heritage.[7] A review meeting was held in December 1993 to assess progress in the implementation of resolutions and to set priorities for future actions.

The conference aimed to identify barriers to access to Australia's documentary heritage, and to establish initiatives and mechanisms that would enable Australians to have the maximum possible bibliographic and physical access to their recorded documentary heritage by the centenary of Australia's Federation in 2001.

The resolutions of the Conference fell into a number of categories. Collecting issues covered some of the current problems of defining the Australian documentary heritage. There were proposals to seek improvements to legal deposit coverage, encourage the sharing of information about collections, and extend our understanding of the difficult concept of national significance. In addition to books and serials, other formats were included for consideration; maps, music, ephemera, pictorial items, audiovisual and electronic materials. Bibliographic issues included the need for better information on current national bibliographical coverage and the development of more detailed action plans based on greater integration of existing bibliographic efforts. One result of this has been a specific project to identify newspaper and journal indexes created by libraries throughout Australia, stage one of which covered the National Library, state and territory libraries, parliamentary libraries, and academic libraries. Stage two is in preparation. Potential bibliographic projects of national significance are being identified for funding. The conference recognized physical access issues and the extent to which practical difficulties inhibit access. Suggestions were made to gain better knowledge of the document supply system and how to use it effectively. Preservation issues focussed on priorities for the recently established National Preservation Office.

Issues relating to special communities were identified, including the difficulties of providing effective library access to Aboriginal and Torres Strait Islanders, multicultural communities, and people with disabilities. Copyright issues included the need for more effective action both at state and federal level in relation to copyright and legal deposit.

ISSUES AND BARRIERS

There are a number of issues that have not been fully resolved concerning the ongoing development of the distributed national collection concept that may have an influence on future developments. Funding is one major issue. Some see it as desirable that libraries should receive special funding to undertake national collecting roles, but in a time of general economic restraint, the potential for any major funding seems limited, not just for collection building, but also for the related functions of control, preservation, and access. The solution here would seem to be judicious use of available funds plus the selection of agreed high priority projects for which special funding could be sought.

Technological developments have been rapid, and their implications are still unknown. There is a need for standards that will facilitate and not inhibit future technological advances. Intellectual property issues have not yet been adequately addressed in this new environment where the concept of fair use seems to be under threat. The contribution of networked information, not available through other means, has still to be defined.

Issues of coordination present challenges, especially among small special libraries, that are not well represented in national decision making forums and whose needs are not fully understood. Such libraries may not choose to recognize that they have a role beyond their own institution and fear that if their holdings are made known they will be overcome by demands for interlibrary loans. The establishment, in 1993, of the Federal Libraries Information Network should enable at least one group of special libraries to have a voice in national decision making.

Other issues are many and varied. What is the relative importance of electronic and paper-based collections, and is this going to change? Should different subject areas (science versus the humanities, for example) be treated differently? Do different formats require different treatments--monographs and serials, for example, not to mention grey literature and ephemera? What are the implications of commercial document suppliers entering the market? Given that the commercial suppliers are all based overseas, what does that mean for national self-sufficiency, and is it important to have materials physically located within the country? Are there other mechanisms which could provide support for the distributed national collection and are existing mechanisms adequate?

CONCLUSION

There is little doubt that the concept of an Australian distributed national collection has provided a focus for thought, discussion and, most importantly, action. In the five years since the notion was formally accepted, there has been an increasing level of commitment to the ideal, not just among libraries but also among politicians and administrators. Practical developments are gradually occurring, assisted by technology and political developments that recognize the need to improve the national information infrastructure. Gradually more mechanisms to support a distributed national collection are being put into place and it would seem that a critical mass of support has now been generated. The opportunity now exists to take advantage of that support and to move further from ideal to reality.

REFERENCES

1. Cultural Ministers' Council, Statistical Advisory Group, *The Australian Cultural Industry: Available Data and Sources*. (Canberra: Australian Government Publishing Service, 1990).

2. National Board of Employment, Education and Training, *Library Provision in Higher Education Institutions*, Commissioned Report Number 7 (Canberra: Australian Government Printing Office, 1991), p. 14.

3. The Parliament of the Commonwealth of Australia, *Australia as an Information Society: The Role of Libraries/Information Networks*, Report of the House of Representatives Standing Committee for Long Term Strategies. (Canberra: Australian Government Printing Office, September 1991), p. 27.

4. *Distinctly Australian: The Future for Australia's Cultural Development*, Australian Labor Party Cultural Policy 1993 Election (Canberra, 1993).

5. *ABN News*, No 70 (July/August 1993), p. 16.

6. Eric Wainwright, "The Distributed National Collection: A View from the Centre," *Australian Library Journal* 40, 3(1991): p. 210-221.

7. *Towards Federation 2001: Linking Australians and Their Heritage*, A National Conference on Access to Australia's Recorded Documentary Heritage. Final Report to which is attached Agenda Papers, Working Papers Background Papers (Canberra: National Library of Australia, 1993).

CENSORSHIP IN ACADEME:
THE NECESSITY FOR VIGILANCE

A. Bruce Strauch

INTRODUCTION

For librarians, censorship is a dirty word. From the very first library school class, librarians learn that censorship is a great enemy and that the people who practice it are not to be emulated. As such, this is a continuing area of interest and concern for all librarians. This paper discusses the possibility for censorship within the academic environment. It also discusses a landmark legal case which has defined censorship in the courts.

Consulting the dictionary for a definition of the word, under the stem "censor" we find the following:

> an official with the power to examine publications, movies, television programs, etc. and to remove or prohibit anything considered obscene, libelous, politically objectionable, etc.[1]

Advances in Collection Development and Resource Management,
Volume 1, pages 153-164.
Copyright © 1995 by JAI Press Inc.
All rights of reproduction in any form reserved.
ISBN: 1-55938-213-9

So we see that librarians, in their role as custodians of information, are in a unique position to influence the nature of that information, or at least the nature of the information which they have available for their constituencies. As such, they may chose to exclude materials from the shelves that may be either controversial or personally objectionable.

SELECTION OR CENSORSHIP

The professional library literature dealing with instances of censorship is voluminous, especially in elementary and secondary public schools.[2] Many articles deal with the efforts of groups, administrators, or those in authority to exclude specific materials from library shelves which are considered objectionable. Whereas the attempt to exclude a specific book may be a clear case of censorship, what is more problematic is the decision not to purchase a particular item because of the content.

This is the kind of subtle censorship that can occur in libraries on a day-to-day basis. And the sophisticated environment of academe is no exception. There is less literature and documentation of censorship in this environment because it is less apparent.[3] However, academic librarians, faculty, bibliographers, and administrators are all in a position to practice censorship on a daily basis.

Just when does selection become censorship? In many cases, this is a fine distinction that only the selector is capable of making because only he or she knows precisely why a specific book or journal is not being chosen for selection.

> Librarians are sometimes accused of censorship because they do not make all reading material equally available to their patrons. This criticism loses sight of the important difference between the censor's negative purpose of denying access to some material and the librarian's positive function of making available as much as possible within his space and budget limitations. The censor rejects, while the librarian selects.[4]

With thousands of books published each year and close to one hundred thousand books in print, libraries simply cannot purchase all materials. Not only is money to purchase the materials scarcer and scarcer, but the shelf space for this volume of material is simply not available. Or how about the volume of gift materials which most libraries receive either through the mails or through interested patrons?

Granted, most libraries have collection development policies which are written to guide the selection of an appropriate body of materials for their user constituency. But most such policies are sufficiently vague to allow considerable discretion in selection.

How can the librarian be sure that he or she is *selecting* rather than *rejecting*? Quite obviously, the line of demarcation between these two terms can be very thin and librarians charged with selection responsibilities must be careful to keep this distinction in mind when making these important decisions.

THEORETICAL BASES

In the First Amendment of the Constitution, our founding fathers wrote:

> Congress shall make no law respecting an establishment of religion, or prohibiting the free exercise thereof; or abridging the freedom of speech or of the press; or the right of the people peaceably to assemble, and to petition the Government for a redress of grievances.[5]

Portions of The Library Bill of Rights, also, speak to these tenets:

> 1. As a responsibility of library service, books and other reading matter selected should be chosen for values of interest, information and enlightenment of all the people for the community. In no case should any book be excluded because of the race or nationality, or the political or religious views of the writer.
> 2. There should be the fullest practicable provision of material presenting all points of view concerning the problems and issues of our times, international, national, and local; and books or other reading matter of sound factual authority should not be proscribed or removed from library shelves because of partisan or doctrinal disapproval.
> 3. Censorship of books ... must be challenged by libraries in maintenance of their responsibility to provide public information and enlightenment through the printed word.[6]

In day-to-day library lives, librarians may not think of these theoretical underpinnings. But they must. By selecting materials for the library's bookshelves, librarians are entering into an important area the integrity of which many before us have sought to preserve.

CASE LAW

The fact that librarians are cognizant of their role in society, of course, obligates them to make themselves aware of what courts of law have said about censorship. This is because, regardless of the best of intentions, there will be those who may put a less than favorable face on the results of selection decisions.

> A popular Government, without popular information, or the means of acquiring it, is but a Prologue to a Farce or a Tragedy; or, perhaps both. Knowledge will forever govern ignorance: And a people who mean to be their own Governors, must arm themselves with the power which knowledge gives.[7]

While few of us may disagree with Madison's moral imperative, how does the hard-pressed librarian deal practically with those few—the reactionary groups that strive to pull books from the shelves which offend their sense of propriety or political rightness, and the far more subtle professor or administrator who defends his or her right to refuse to purchase certain materials?

As in cases where there is dispute, we all tend to look to some higher authority. What can we glean from legal opinions to guide us? Unfortunately, the law is seldom cut and dried. And with censorship, despite an abundance of talk and public debate, there have been few cases. These cases are further limited to their particular set of facts. Indeed, since the cases deal with public school libraries rather than higher education and with specific book titles rather than with broad ideological concepts, we may mistakenly think them irrelevant. This is untrue. When the courts speak to an issue as nebulous and charged as censorship we must make ourselves aware of the facts so that we can draw some conclusions that will guide professional librarians.

The U.S. Supreme Court has spoken most significantly on the issue of censorship in the landmark *Board of Education, Island Trees*

Union Free School District No. 26, et al. v. *Pico,* 457 U.S. Reports 853, 102 S.Ct. Reporter 2799 (1982). (hereafter referred to as Island Trees). Simply stated, *Island Trees* held that local school boards may not remove books from school libraries merely because they find ideas presented in those books objectionable.

It all began when, in 1975, a conservative parent organization presented to a school board in Long Island, New York a list of nine books it found to be objectionable. The books were all famous: *Slaughter House Five*, by Kurt Vonnegut, Jr.; *The Naked Ape*, by Desmond Morris; *Down These Means Streets*, by Piri Thomas; *Best Short Stories of Negro Writers*, edited by Langston Hughes; *Go Ask Alice*, of anonymous authorship; *Laughing Boy*, by Oliver LaFarge; *Black Boy*, by Richard Wright; *A Hero Ain't Nothin' But A Sandwich*, by Alice Childress; and *Soul On Ice*, by Eldridge Cleaver.

To those of us familiar with these books, it may be shocking to know that The School Board directed the school principal to remove the books from the library for review as to their suitability. Subsequently, a parents' committee studied the books and recommended that only two of the nine be permanently removed. The School Board rejected their position and removed all nine books, stating that they were "anti-American, anti-Christian, anti-Semitic and just plain filthy."

So it was that suit was brought by Steven Pico and other high school students in Federal District Court. The Plaintiffs alleged the violation of their First Amendment rights. The First Amendment has been applied to the states by the Fourteenth Amendment and in the well-known *Gitlow* v. *New York*, 268 U.S. 652, 666 (1925). What this means is that state government as well as federal shall not abridge freedom of speech or of the press.

Since a school board is a state organ, it is subject to suit on such issues. As *Island Trees* unfolded in the U.S. Supreme Court, briefs of amici curiae by parties against the books' removal were filed by such organizations as the AFL-CIO, the American Library Association, the Anti-Defamation League of B'Nai B'Rith, the Association of American Publishers, Inc., and the National Education Association.

At trial, The School Board conceded that the books in question were not obscene. Obscenity has been held to be properly kept from minors in *Ginsberg* v. *New York*, 390 U.S. 629, 88 S.Ct. 1274, 20 L.Ed.2d 195 (1968). Thus, The Board had modified its position somewhat, contending that the books were "irrelevant, vulgar, immoral, and in bad taste, making them educationally unsuitable" for the students. Vulgarity, while a lesser standard than obscenity, is nonetheless all the more nebulous and difficult to identify.

However, the District Court granted judgment for The School Board, finding that it had broad discretion in the formulation of educational policy. It cited *Presidents Council, District 25* v. *Community School Board No. 25,* 457 F.2d 289 (CA2 1972); *James* v. *Board of Education,* 461 F.2d 566,573 (CA2 1972); *East Hartford Educational Assn.* v. *Board of Education,* 562 F.2d 838, 856 (CA2 1977).

Courts, the District Court held, should not interfere with school system operations unless "basic constitutional values" were involved, and this situation did not exist. Removing books for vulgarity might be misguided but did not infringe the First Amendment rights of the students.

Subsequent to this, in 1980, the U.S. Court of Appeals for the Second Circuit reversed the decision in *Island Trees*, and the U.S. Supreme Court granted certiorari in 1981, hearing the case in that year.

At the outset of the opinion, the Supreme Court emphasized that its holding (opinion) was limited and did not concern the acquisition of books for the library. It only concerned the removal of books already in place on the shelves.

Further, the case did not involve compulsory courses and readings taught in the classroom since local school boards have broad discretion in this area.[8] Though the Court struck down state statutes prohibiting the teaching of modern languages in the first case and the Darwinian theory in the second, it emphasized that school boards should be allowed to create curriculum in such a way as to teach community values. Schools have a legitimate function of "inculcating fundamental values necessary to the maintenance of a democratic political system."[9] Nonetheless, as shown by the holdings, fundamental values of free speech and inquiry will be safeguarded.

Further, in other court rulings, students were not to leave their constitutional rights at the school house door. *West Virginia Board of Education* v. *Barnette*, 319 U.S. 624 (1943) held students could not be compelled to salute the flag, and *Tinker* v. *Des Moines School Dist.*, 393 U.S. 503 (1969) protected students' right to wear black armbands to protest the Vietnam War, a form of symbolic free speech. The School Board's claimed fear of disturbance in *Tinker* was not sufficient reason to prevent free expression.

> Any departure from absolute regimentation may cause trouble. Any variation from the majority's opinion may inspire fear. Any word spoken, in class, in the lunchroom, or on the campus, that deviates from the views of another person may start an argument or cause a disturbance. But our Constitution says we must take this risk ... and our history says that it is this sort of hazardous freedom—this kind of openness—that is the basis of our national strength and of the independence and vigor of Americans who grow up and live in this ... often disputatious society.[10]

In keeping with the cases, the Island Trees School Board argued that they were transmitting community values by the removal of the books and should have absolute discretion in these actions. Library use, however, the Court noted, was voluntary on the part of the students. It was a place of self-education and individual study and intellectual growth.

Here we enter a troublesome area. School Boards have a substantial legitimate role in determining the books in the library. That role ceases to be legitimate if they become involved in the suppression of ideas.

> If there is any fixed star in our constitutional constellation, it is that no official, high or petty, can prescribe what shall be orthodox in politics, nationalism, religion, or other matters of opinion .... If there are any circumstances which permit an exception, they do not now occur to us.[11]

While this quotation is drawn from the compulsory flag saluting case, it was interpreted in *Island Trees* to mean that school boards should not be motivated by a desire to deny students access to ideas with which the school board disagreed. This would be an attempt to prescribe what is orthodox in politics, nationalism, religion. And the state should not be trying to create "a homogeneous people."[12]

Returning to *Island Trees*, the Court found, however, that it would not be unconstitutional for the Board to remove books because (1) they were pervasively vulgar; or because of (2) "educational unsuitability."

In reviewing the evidence of the intent of The School Board in the book removal, the Court noted that the Board claimed to have removed the books because they were "anti-American, contained obscenities, blasphemies, brutality, and perversion beyond description." This would seem to be in line with the majority holding.

However, the Board had no review policy for controversial materials and ignored the advice of literary experts, librarians, and school district teachers. The Court found that the books were in fact removed because they were on a list of books found objectionable by a parents' group.

To recap the Court's holding in *Island Trees*, while school boards can ban books that are educationally unsuitable or pervasively vulgar, they must not actively attempt to subvert ideas through the library acquisition of materials.

The Dissent

Chief Justice Burger along with Justices Powell, Rehnquist, and O'Connor dissented in the *Island Trees* decision. Under the narrow ruling of the Court, a school board could choose not to buy a book for any reason whatsoever. But once purchased, the book had to remain in the collection until a reason could be found for its removal. Is the official suppression greater when a book is removed than when it is never purchased in the first place?

First, the dissenters addressed the possibility that the right not to have books removed might potentially carry a concommitant right to have books purchased. Their fear was of opening a potential floodgate of litigation over materials acquisition when libraries were already strapped with limited budgets. Every library cannot be the Library of Congress. Authors should not be allowed to claim a constitutional right to have their books in libraries.

[E]ducators must separate the relevant from the irrelevant, the appropriate from the inappropriate. Determining what information not to present to the students is often as important as identifying relevant materials. This winnowing process necessarily leaves much information to be discovered by students at another time or in another place.[13]

What right, the dissent asked, does anyone really have to remove ideas from a library's bookshelves if the school board determines certain books are inappropriate or irrelevant to the school's curriculum? Books are available from stores unconnected with the public schools. Ideas which are readily available elsewhere have not been suppressed by the state.

Next the dissenting justices criticized the broad language of the phrases "educationally unsuitable" and "pervasively vulgar." As guidelines permitting the removal of books, the dissenting judges found them impossible to apply.

"Educational suitability" ... is a standardless phrase. This conclusion will undoubtedly be drawn in many—if not most—instances because of the decisionmaker's content-based judgment that the ideas contained in the book or the idea expressed from the author's method of communication are inappropriate for teenage pupils.[14]

Further, the dissenting judges continued: Vulgarity is something short of obscenity, and obscenity has been difficult enough for the nation to determine. But what is "pervasive vulgarity"? Pervasive is defined by *Webster's New International Dictionary of the English Language* (2nd Ed., Unabridged) as "widespread." Is it ever possible that the vulgarity found in one chapter or on one page is of such substantial vulgarity that it is worse than pervasive?

In short, the dissent seemed to feel that schools should have almost unlimited discretion in the selection of library materials. Any meddling in this by the courts would lead to persistent litigation and create insurmountable difficulties for libraries in selecting materials on limited budgets.

PRACTICAL REALITIES

What, if anything, does all this legalese mean for the practicing college librarian? First and foremost, state institutions of higher education clearly fall under the same rules as state secondary schools. In state institutions, college librarians must be as alert to the censorship problem and the potential for annoying litigation as the public school librarian.

Second, the fear of the dissent in Island Trees—that courts will find that an author has a constitutional right to have a work included in a collection—may seem unrealistic. However, it would probably be safe to say, that if books cannot be removed because of the ideas they contain, an institution cannot refuse to purchase books for the same reason.

Therefore, any library would be well advised to have a detailed collection development policy that is clearly linked to the institution's curriculum or research objectives. Such a policy, as librarians have been repeatedly taught, provides a reasonable defense against attacks by pressure groups both inside and outside the institution.

Third, personal prejudices are going to necessarily enter into the selection of books. Faculty competition for limited funds and campus infighting may well result in irritating accusations of censorship. Finger-pointing and wild accusations based on the bare evidence of the exclusion of one book or a few books does not constitute a showing of censorship.

Understanding that censorship means book selection in such a way as to exclude unpopular ideas, the librarian's defense lies in requiring coolly and calmly that evidence be presented to show such a systematic policy.

CONCLUSION

In 1986, Elizabeth Hood of Trinity University Library did a study of library selectors using a controversial book, *Let Me Die Before I Wake: Hemlock's Guide to Self-Deliverance for the Dying* by Derek Humphry. She asked them whether or not they would add the book to the library's shelves and she attempted to investigate the reasons behind each selector's decision.[15] Alarmingly, Hood found that subjectivity in selection of this particular title was the rule rather than the exception. And, unfortunately, Hood's results are not that unusual. How many make similar decisions unhampered by the scrutiny of a conscientious colleague?

Table 1. Possible Checklist for Selection

— Does your library have a collection development policy?
— Does the material come under selection guidelines in your collection development policy?
— Do you agree or disagree with the views expressed in the material?
— If you agree, are you selecting the material simply because you agree with it?
— If you disagree, are you not selecting the material simply you disagree with it?
— Can you defend your decision to a third party?

Though the technique used by Hood is not practical for those charged with overseeing selection, it should nonetheless cause selectors to stop and pause. When the library chooses not to purchase a book or journal, it is depriving all but the most tenacious of patrons access to the material. Conversely, when a library purchases a book or journal, it is exposing it to a wider audience of patrons. So librarians must, in each case, check the reasons behind decisions. (See Table 1 for a possible checklist.) Librarians must be sure that they are not so much rejecting a book or journal as they are selecting materials for their user constituency. It is their responsibility as librarians. As Lester Asheim so aptly put it many years ago,

the aim of the selector is to promote reading, not to inhibit it; to multiply the points of view which will find expression, not limit them; to be a channel for communication, not a bar against it.[16]

Theoretical and legal bases notwithstanding, we all have our own opinions and prejudices. These opinions and prejudices shape selection decisions that librarians make on a day-to-day basis either consciously or unconsciously. To deny this is to be unrealistic.

To recognize this is to accept the role of libraries and librarians. As the repositories of society's information, libraries, and so librarians, play an invaluable role. Each day in selection decisions, librarians are playing a small role in what will be remembered of our society.

NOTES AND REFERENCES

1. *Webster's New World Dictionary of the American Language*, Second College Edition (New York: The World Publishing Company, 1972), p. 230.

2.   One of the most complete recent treatments of censorship in the public schools is *Battle of the Books: Literary Censorship in the Public Schools, 1950-1985,* by Lee Burress, (Metuchen, NJ: Scarecrow, 1989).

3.   There are some exceptions. See, for example, Elizabeth Hood, "Academic Library Censorship in a Conservative Era," in *Energies for Transition, Proceedings of the Fourth National Conference of the Association of College and Research Libraries, Baltimore, MD, April 9-12* (Chicago: ALA/ACRL, 1986), pp. 15-17.

4.   *The Censorship of Books*, edited by Walter M. Daniels (New York: H.W. Wilson, 1954), p. 3.

5.   *The Constitution of the United States of America*, Amendment I, ratification completed December 15, 1791.

6.   From "The Library Bill of Rights", adopted by Council of the American Library Association (1939).

7.   *Writings of James Madison*, vol. 9, edited by G. Hunt (New York: 1910), p. 103.

8.   See *Meyer* v. *Nebraska*, 262 U.S. 390 (1923) and *Epperson* v. *Arkansas*, 393 U.S. 97 (1968).

9.   See *Ambach* v. *Norwick*, 441 U.S. 68, 77 (1979).

10.   *Tinker* v. *Des Moines School Dist.*, supra at 508-509.

11.   *West Virginia Board of Education* v. *Barnette*, 319 U.S., at 642.

12.   *Tinker* v. *Des Moines School Dist.*, 393 U.S., at 511.

13.   *Island Trees*, at 914.

14.   *Island Trees*, at 890.

15.   Hood, "Academic Library Censorship."

16.   Lester Asheim, "Not Censorship But Selection," *Wilson Library Bulletin* 28 (September 1953): 68.

SELECTED BIBLIOGRAPHY

Berninghausen, David K. *The Flight From Reason, Essays on Intellectual Freedom in the Academy, the Press, and the Library.* Chicago: American Library Association, 1975.

Bosmajian, Haig, Comp. *Censorship, Libraries, and the Law.* New York: Neal-Shuman, 1983.

Daniels, Walter M., Ed., *Censorship of Books.* (The Reference Shelf, vol. 26, No. 5.) New York: H.W. Wilson, 1954.

Energies for Transition, Proceedings of the Fourth National Conference of the Association of College and Research Libraries, April 9-12 , 1986, Baltimore, Maryland. Chicago: ALA/ACRL, 1986.

Hauptman, Robert. *Ethical Challenges in Librarianship.* Phoenix, AZ: Oryx Press, 1988.

Hoffman, Frank. *Intellectual Freedom and Censorship.* Metuchen, NJ: Scarecrow, 1989.

COMPUTER AND INFORMATION
SYSTEM WARRANTIES:
CAVEAT EMPTOR

J. Michael Alford and A. Bruce Strauch

INTRODUCTION

Efforts to increase productivity and profitability both in the factory
and the office have led to significant investments in automated
manufacturing technology and computer technology by U.S.
businesses. A 1988 survey indicated that over 60 percent of U.S.
companies expected to increase their computer hardware expenditures
during the next year continues.[1] In the software area, 39 percent
expected to increase expenditures. These investments range from
relatively simple word processing systems to complex systems including
Computer-Integrated-Manufacturing (CIM) systems and information
systems designed to handle worldwide financial transaction data.

Advances in Collection Development and Resource Management,
Volume 1, pages 165-176.
Copyright © 1995 by JAI Press Inc.
All rights of reproduction in any form reserved.
ISBN: 1-55938-213-9

What all of these systems have in common is that they depend upon properly designed software and reliable hardware to ensure the success of projects. Another common factor is that the increased use of computer technology carries with it an increased risk on the part of the user. This risk results from the demand from the user for equipment and software that can provide more complex functions than available earlier and the desire of the producers of equipment and software to sell their products in a very competitive market. All firms, large and small, are at risk. Also, the larger producers seem to have as many problems as the smaller producers in terms of providing satisfactory hardware and software.

Additionally, the user is typically dependent on the expertise of the vendor in areas ranging form identification of needs to installation and checkout of the systems. In some cases the hardware vendor has the software prepared by independent software firms. Some of the software firms may consist of only one person. In other instances, the user decides on both the hardware vendor and the software source.

To set the stage for developing strategies that should reduce the risk to the user and help ensure a successful implementation, some pertinent factors of contract law and warranties are presented. Additionally, some actual events in warranty situations are provided as illustrations of areas of concern or potential problems that the user may be able to avoid by using the recommended strategies.

CONTRACT LAW

Let the buyer beware in all sales of computer equipment. Three basic areas of contract law confine the buyer to the narrowly-constructed written document and eliminate all outside promises.

1. The Statute of Frauds requires that there be a written contract.
2. The Parol Evidence Rule eliminates all outside promises and representations as to quality and performance.
3. The writing itself will limit warranties and remedies.

Goods are defined by the Uniform Commercial Code (UCC) as "anything which is moveable." As such, all computer hardware and software are goods and fall under section 2 of the code.

The Statute of Frauds, which dates from the time of Henry VIII and is codified as Sec. 36-2-201, was intended to keep lying contests out of the courtroom by requiring written contracts for all important commercial transactions. Sec. 36-2-201 provides:

> (1) ... a contract for the sale of goods for the price of $500 or more is not enforceable by way of action or defense unless there is some writing sufficient to indicate that a contract for sale has been made between the parties and signed by the party against whom enforcement is sought or by his authorized agent or broker.

The practical effect of this would be for the parties to a handshake agreement to be procedurally thrown out of the courtroom if the buyer breached the contract by not buying and the seller tried to sue him. While it is possible to have a handshake agreement and get into the courtroom on a breach, one side must have delivered. Either the equipment must have been received and accepted or the check handed to the vendor. This so-called "part performance" exception is found in Sec. 36-2-201(3)(c).

A contract that does not satisfy the requirements of subsection (1), but which is valid in other respects is enforceable with respect to goods for which payment has been made and accepted or which have been received and accepted. In fact, a situation where the buyer has accepted the goods of an oral contract of sale but has yet to pay because of dissatisfaction with quality, the vendor could sue. However, without a written agreement, the buyer could present as oral testimony any claim of promised quality or performance which he wished. He might be scrupulously honest or a bald-faced liar, yet all testimony would come before the jury.

From the vendor's perspective, this is a disaster. The jury would most likely side with the "little guy" against the big household name computer companies. Further, juries, schooled on the magical computers of television and movie dramas, would tend to believe that computers, currently at a relatively crude stage of development, should perform like Luke Skywalker's Star Wars mode.

By the vendor's realizing the necessity of a written contract, the buyer is put at his first disadvantage. The second disadvantage arises from the Parol Evidence Rule, Sec. 36-2-201 Final written expression; parol or extrinsic evidence:

Terms with respect to which the confirmatory memoranda of the parties or which are otherwise set forth in a writing intended by the parties as a final expression of their agreement with respect to such terms as are included therein may not be contradicted by evidence of any prior agreement or of a contemporaneous oral agreement.

Parol Evidence is simply oral testimony, the word parol coming from the medieval French verb *paroler*—to speak—which in its modern form is *parler*. The point of the parol evidence rule is that a writing is assumed to be the final agreement of the parties. As buyer and seller are logically expected to read and understand what they sign, all important elements of the contract ought to be included. Consequently, any oral agreements simultaneous with or prior to the written agreement are not admissible as evidence at trial. The writing alone will be examined by the trier of fact.

Thus, any promises by the vendor as to quality or performance made along with the sale are not admissible in evidence if they are not included in the writing. The unwary buyer will be consistently gulled by the vendor's sales patter and machine gun stream of promises and will find to his despair that they are not included in the writing. He will discover this long after the fact when some of the oral promises have been breached and he has really studied the contract for the first time.

WARRANTIES

Warranties are vendor's promises as to quality or performance which become a part of the basis of the bargain. Express warranties are created by explicit representation; implied warranties arise by law. It is in the vendor's best interest to define his promises carefully within the writing and to eliminate the vagueness of the implied warranties altogether.

A typical, almost industry-standard express warranty might be as follows:

Limited Warranty
The hardware furnished hereunder is warranted to be free from defects in material and workmanship for a period of ninety (90) days from the date of installation

for X ___ Corp. for seller installed hardware, and ninety (90) days from the date of delivery for Customer installed hardware.

Limited Warranty
The software is warranted to conform to X ___ Corp's (seller's) published specifications.

Limitation of Remedies

In addition to the exclusion of warranties, a typical contract will contain several limitations of the remedies available to the buyer. For example:

> X ___ Corp will, at its own expense and option, either repair or replace defective hardware, provided the customer has notified X ___ Corp and upon inspection X——— Corp has found such hardware to b defective. The customer's sole and exclusive remedy hereunder will be limited to such repair or replacement.

or

> The sole remedies for breach of any and all warranties and the sole remedies for X ___ Corp (seller) liability of any kind with respect to the products or service provided hereunder and any other performance by X ___ Corp under or pursuant to the agreement shall be limited to the remedies provided in the applicable warranty paragraphs hereof. In on event shall X ___ Corp's liability to the customer for damages of any nature exceed the total charges paid or payable for services during one (1) year under this agreement if the liability arises from service, or the purchase price of the product(s) if the liability results therefrom.

The following example is extracted from the license agreement on a software package from WordPerfect Corporation.

> In no way will WPCORP be liable to you for damages, including any loss of profits, lost savings, or other incidental or consequential damages arising out of your use or inability to the program, even if WPCORP or an authorized WPCORP representative has been advised of the possibility of such damages, or for any claim by any other party.

In addition, there will typically be an exclusion of all other warranties than the published specs as follows: THE EXPRESS WARRANTIES SET FORTH IN THE AGREEMENT ARE IN

LIEU OF ALL OTHER WARRANTIES, EXPRESS OR IMPLIED INCLUDING WITHOUT LIMITATION ANY WARRANTIES OF MERCHANTABILITY OR FITNESS FOR A PARTICULAR PURPOSE.

The Implied Warranty of Merchantability UCC Sec. 36-2-314 requires that goods be "merchantable," which means that should "pass without objection in the trade" and "be fit for the ordinary purposes for which the goods are used." This marvelously vague standard is designed to protect the buyer. If the implied warranty were applicable, the buyer could go into the courtroom and testify as to any and all oral promises of the vendor, offering this as proof of what "passes in the trade". It is essential that the vendor prevent this by the warranty disclaimer.

EXAMPLES

Three examples presented here cover a span of 14 years and are situations that resulted in actual court cases. However, in speaking with business people who have installed or are in the process of installing computer technology, it is not uncommon to hear that the installation went according to schedule insofar as hardware is concerned, but the software applications will not perform the tasks envisioned by the user without considerable modification.

A recent case encountered by one of the authors involved a small manufacturing firm that installed an operating system which would track and report upon productivity and inventory. This was a make-to-order job shop. The manager was concerned about the large variances between the results provided by the system and the physical inventory. In some cases the variance was 100 percent. Investigation revealed the variance was caused because two major customers required that their own stock numbers be assigned to goods once they were in the manufacturing process, however, there was no way in the system to automatically account for this change. This situation resulted because of a misunderstanding of what the system vendor thought the user wanted and the user's lack of understanding of the limitations of the system. Fortunately, an expensive software rewrite and legal action were avoided by providing instructions to the operators on how to enter data in a fashion that would adjust the inventory balances to reflect decreases on stock inventory and conversion to a new stock number. This did require two additional entries by the operators, but it was a minor inconvenience compared to the time and expense involved in other solutions.

What Happens When You Go to Court? Three Examples

On June 19, 1989, a trial got underway in Clearwater, Florida which promised to have a major impact on vendor liability no matter what the outcome. Because of the importance of such networks to many businesses, it situation was closely watched by both users and vendors. At issue was whether network vendors should be liable when a user loses business due to equipment or service problems. Home Shopping Network, Inc. (HSN) sued GTE for $1.5 billion for fraud and misrepresentation, saying that network equipment and services provided by GTE failed to operate as promised, causing HSN to lose $500 million in business.

According to attorneys, providers of network equipment and services are generally limited in their liability. A user typically can recover only the cost of the service or equipment that fails to work properly, and not damages for business losses. In this instance, GTE filed a $100 million counter suit charging HSN with besmirching its reputation in order to save its own slumping business.[2] The cases were tried simultaneously. The results were that HSN lost the lawsuit in August of 1989 and was to make an undisclosed cash payment to GTE.[3] HSN appealed the results. In November, HSN announced that all claims arising from the lawsuit had been settled. In December, it was revealed that the HSN had paid $4.5 million in cash to GTE.[4]

The troubles for HSN management did not end there. Stockholders filed a class action suit against HSN and seven of its directors claiming that the suit against GTE Corporation was intended to divert blame from HSN's mediocre financial performance.[5]

An Illinois court dismissed class action suits brought by network users against Illinois Bell Telephone Company for business losses in the wake of the disastrous Hinsdale, Illinois, central office fire in May 1988.[6]

The *Badger Bearing Co.* v. *Burroughs Corp.*, 444 F. Suppl. 919 (E.D) Wis.1977) case reveals another horror story for the buyer. Burroughs came to the buyer with the following written proposal:

> We recommend that you install a Burroughs E6000 Computer. This machine will be used on the applications we discussed a few days ago in our bound portfolio. These are:
>
> 1. Billing with Automatic Up-dating of Accounts Receivable;
> 2. Inventory Up-Dating;
> 3. Inventory Stock Status Report;
> 4. Inventory Nonactivity List;
> 5. Inventory Listing by Product;
> 6. Inventory Listing by Mfg. by Product;
> 7. Customer Analysis by Salesman by Dollars by Product Bought
> 8. Monthly Age Analysis by Customer.
>
> After reviewing your present system and requirements for a proposed system, we are confident that the installation of a Burroughs E6000 Computer will afford you:
> MORE WORK IN LESS TIME AND MORE MEANINGFUL MANAGEMENT INFORMATION THAN EVER BEFORE POSSIBLE.

To the buyer's later chagrin, this writing did NOT become part of the final contract. Rather, the buyer signed the standard contract with disclaimer warranties. The buyer was given a three-month repair warranty. The buyer suffered an average of one mechanical breakdown per week. Seventy-six service calls were made. The buyer had to pay extensive overtime to his employees due to delays in billing caused by the defective system. Four of the eight applications could not be made to work at all.

The Court in *Badger* found that the Burroughs contract effectively disclaimed warranties and that the written proposal was not a part of the contract. The buyer had simply failed to read and understand his contract and his mistake was a unilateral one which he, as a reasonable buyer, should not have made.

To the typical buyer, such a situation is a financial disaster. A computer malfunction brings his business to a halt. The consequential damages of a work slow-down or destroyed records are far greater than any costs of repair. The buyer would reasonably expect to be made whole for such injuries. What the buyer will find in his contract are the limitations of remedies mentioned in the warranties section above.

The typical agreement between the parties contains three separate limitations of remedies available to the buyer. The first is that repair or replacement of defective equipment is the exclusive remedy. The second is that the seller's liability is limited to the price paid for the defective part. Finally, the buyer cannot recover for any special, incidental, indirect or consequential damages or for the loss of profit, revenue, or data. The Code permits this limitation of remedies in Sec. 36-2-316(4).

STRATEGIES FOR THE BUYER

Computer systems are typically purchased to increase productivity and profitability. Therefore, it is important to make an up-front investment of time and energy, and even money, to:

1. *Find out your needs and what is available to satisfy those needs.*

   - Identify your needs; current and future.
   - Develop some systems expertise in house or find a competent consultant.
   - Study vendor proposals carefully.
   - Request that the vendor identify (in writing) exactly how the product will satisfy your needs (put it in any purchase Contract or agreement also).
   - Find out what training is available and the costs.
   - Find out what software options are available.
   - Talk to more than one vendor.
   - Get information on several systems.
   - Can the vendor(s) refer you to similar businesses which
   - Can verify what you are hearing from the vendor(s)?

2. *Understand the warranties.*

    - What is covered for hardware?
    - What is covered for software?
    - What are the exclusions and limitations of remedy?
    - Is local service available?
    - What are the procedures for obtaining service?
    - How long will warranty remedy continue once corrective action is started?

3. *The warranty is part of the contract. The contract should be agreeable to both parties.*

    - Request written clarification before you sign. (Remember oral promises are worthless after a contract is signed.)
    - Request what you think are reasonable changes to contract language or stipulations.

Several similar approaches to purchasing computer equipment have been recommended over the years, and they apply to firms ranging from small-size to the largest firms. Karasik recommends that one choose software first and hardware last. He also provides a checklist aimed at helping the potential purchaser choose the appropriate vendor.[7] *Inc.* magazine established a Computer Dealers Advisory Panel for the purpose of developing advice for computer buyers. The panel of experts developed a checklist that is useful to both first time buyers and those updating systems.[8] The article also presents some ideas for looking into the warranty aspect of the purchase and contains specific advice based on the experiences of individual panel members.

Post-Purchase Actions

The computer buyer may avoid a number of pitfalls, headaches, frustrations, and loss of money by utilizing the information above when arranging to purchase equipment and software. However, sometimes the results obtained from a system are much less than expected. When this occurs the buyer sometimes is tempted to throw out the system and sue the vendor. There are a number of factors to consider before taking this drastic action.

For example, can the firm afford the loss in time and investment of starting over? Is there an alternative supplier available who can provide what you need if you throw out the present system? What are the chances of a successful lawsuit? As a result of investigating this matter, Raysman and Brown recommend that in some instances a negotiated settlement with the vendor may be the best approach for both the user and the vendor.[9] They suggest a "structured negotiating approach" that involves seeking expert assistance, defining issues, examination of the agreement, involvement of top management, presentation of detailed demands to the vendor, negotiation, and then drawing up an agreement to remedy the problems.

SUMMARY

There are many approaches to buying computer equipment and systems. They range from mail order to custom installations. From a strategic standpoint, it is imperative that the potential buyer invest time, effort, and money in understanding the needs for the immediate future and the long term. The user should realize that it may take months to find the correct solution to the needs that are identified. The user should not leave the identification of needs up to the vendor. Do not rush into a great sounding deal. Talk to other users in your industry; there are user groups ranging from accounting procedure interests up to and including manufacturing systems. These people are willing to share information with you. Develop a specific contact person within your organization for dealing with vendors. This is particularly important for major installations. You may need to establish a project team. Remember that your business and perhaps your personal future may be at risk when you transition to a computer supported operation.

REFERENCES

1. *Datamation* (February 5, 1988): 106.
2. Bob Brown, "HSN-GTE Lawsuit Could Set Vendor Liability Precedent," *Network World* (June 19, 1989): 2, 69.

3.   Wayne Eckerson, "HSN Loses $1.5b GTE Suit, Must Pay $100m Damages," *Datamation* (August 7, 1989): 4.

4.   *News Week* (December 18, 1989).

5.   "TOP NEWS; Briefs," *Datamation* (December 18, 1989): 2.

6.   "TOP NEWS; Briefs," *Datamation* (August 14,1989): 2.

7.   Myron S. Karasik, "Selecting a Small Business Computer," *Harvard Business Review* (January-February 1984): 26-30.

8.   "How to Get the Best From a Computer Dealer," *Inc.* (November 1987): 157-185.

9.   Richard Raysman and P. Brown, "Don't Rush to Court When Your Computer Fails," *Harvard Business Review* (January-February 1984): 118-124.

EDUCATION FOR ACQUISITIONS

William Fisher

INTRODUCTION

While holiday shopping, I came across the following greeting card. On the cover were three illustrations: (1) a goofy-looking guy captioned "This is Manny"; (2) a stopwatch captioned "This is Manny's watch"; (3) and a scale (like the scales used in Westerns to measure gold) captioned "This is Manny's scale." At the bottom of the cover the caption read, "Nobody knows exactly what Manny does with these objects ...." Open the card and the caption continues "... Although its been said Manny times, Manny weighs ... Merry Christmas!" Beyond demonstrating my tolerance for bad jokes, I relate the story of Manny because as I began to consider the question of library school education for acquisitions it occurred to me that it has been said "Manny times, Manny weighs" that library schools are not doing enough to prepare people to perform the acquisitions

Advances in Collection Development and Resource Management,
Volume 1, pages 177-185.
Copyright © 1995 by JAI Press Inc.
All rights of reproduction in any form reserved.
ISBN: 1-55938-213-9

function in libraries and information centers. This has clearly been
the case for the past twenty-five years or so, as the literature would
indicate, and the debate in one form or another goes back even
further.[1]

THE DEBATE CIRCA 1978

While the arguments and counterarguments for greater attention to
acquisitions in the library school curriculum have not changed much
over the years, there was a good review of the discussion in 1978
through a series of four articles in *Library Acquisitions: Practice and
Theory*. The first article by William Myrick discusses the imperfection
of library education in general and the inadequacy of education for
acquisitions.[2] Myrick also sets the tone by defining acquisitions as the
functions involved in procuring library material rather than selecting
it, although he notes it is not possible to make a 100 percent clear
distinction. Finally, Myrick proposes what topics should be included
in a course dealing with acquisitions, based upon what he has found
to be important working as an acquisitions librarian.

The next article was by Nancy Williamson, then an Associate
Professor at Toronto's library school.[3] Williamson used a definition
similar to Myrick, looking at acquisitions primarily from a
procurement viewpoint. She presented the results of a survey she
conducted among the accredited library schools in North America
to determine where acquisitions fit into the curricular "scheme of
things." Two of Williamson's results are interesting to note: (1) of
the sixty-four accredited programs at that time only twenty-eight
(44%) of the schools responded (you can make of that what you wish);
and (2) only two of the responding schools provided evidence of a
separate course in acquisitions and put the topic well within the
context of the definitions used by both Williamson and Myrick. The
predominate curricular structure that Williamson noted was the
teaching of acquisitions in a couple of class sessions within the
framework of some other course, and most of these courses were not
required for all MLS students to take.

The third article was by Judith Serebnick, then an Assistant
Professor at Indiana.[4] Serebnick joined the fray by trying to answer

the fairly direct question: Are Library Schools Educating Acquisitions Librarians? As the other authors did, Serebnick began with some definitions: (1) that the MLS program is but "part of a librarian's continuing professional education,"[5] which means MLS programs aren't designed to do everything; and second, that acquisitions is "concerned with selecting, ordering, and receiving materials"[6] in response to the interests of a library's community. In this second definition, Serebnick has just expanded the milieu of acquisitions to include selection, community analysis, and user studies (among other topics), which Myrick and Williamson excluded from their definitions. This allowed Serebnick to primarily discuss library education within the context of these latter issues, rather than procurement of materials, and that picture looked a lot "rosier" than the ones presented by either Myrick or Williamson. So, what was Serebnick's answer? As any good academic would, she does not actually give one. Based on her definition of acquisitions, Serebnick felt many of the elements of acquisitions were part of library school curriculums at that time. However, she went on to say that the only way to know for sure would be a thorough evaluation of course content and library school graduates' performance as acquisitions librarians.

The last of the four articles dealt with "formalizing" preparation for acquisitions work.[7] In this article, Sara Heitshu discussed acquisitions education at the University of Michigan's library school. At that time "Building Library Collections," was a required course that introduced acquisitions to all students in the program. A more rigorous examination of the acquisitions process appeared to come in a course on technical services, which was not required. Heitshu also described Michigan's Graduate Student Staff Assistant program, a cooperative effort between the library school and the university library system. This program allowed students to work in various units of the library and go to library school. University of Michigan's Book Purchasing Division was an active participant in the program, acquainting students with its activities. Heitshu concludes her article with a brief mention about other ways of providing acquisitions experience to both students and professionals. These included student jobs and internships in acquisitions departments, local networking efforts of acquisitions librarians, and national activities primarily through ALA divisions and committees.

THE DEBATE CIRCA 1991

Much of this debate was repeated in 1991, when the education issue was brought up by the Association for Library Collections and Technical Services at the ALA Midwinter Conference. This time the two sides of the issue were presented by Joyce Ogburn and Deanna Marcum. Ogburn, collection development support librarian at Yale, defended the idea of acquisitions in the library school curriculum based on "its theory, its special knowledge base, its unique research perspective, and the value to the profession as a whole of having acquisitions in the curriculum."[8] Marcum, then the dean of Catholic University's School of Library and Information Science, offered four reasons why library schools would not respond with a separate acquisitions course.[9] Marcum's concerns were: (1) the problem of the duration of most MLS programs makes it possible to include only so much in any one student's program; (2) since the profession as a whole has not identified specifically what any MLS graduate should know, library schools need to prepare students for any of the four traditional environments; (3) the current "generation" of students appears to have a more definite idea of what courses they want to take and what they want to get out of those courses; and (4) the job market is too unstable to allow students to "specialize" during library school with any certainty of finding employment in that specialization. Marcum concludes that, "a combination of all these factors makes it difficult for the library school to insert new required courses into the curriculum".[10]

From this it appears as though little had changed from the late 1970s into this decade. This view was confirmed to some degree or another by four separate studies conducted recently. The first of these studies was by Karen Schmidt, acquisitions librarian at the University of Illinois.[11] Schmidt surveyed acquisitions librarians working in member libraries of the Association of Research Libraries (ARL). The respondents were asked a series of questions, two of which are of primary interest for our purposes. Schmidt broke the acquisitions function down into fifteen tasks and asked for each task what proportion of their education did the respondents receive from each of five sources. The sources of education included library school, on-the-job training, workshops/conferences, vendors, and other (with the respondent specifying what other meant). She then asked, for the same fifteen tasks, where education *should* come from among those same five sources. The aggregate response for where their education *did* come from included: on-the-job training (78%), workshops/conferences (8%), library school (5%), vendors (5%), and other (4%). The response to where education *should* come from included: on-the-job training (58%), library school (26%), workshops/conferences (10%), vendors (3%), and other (2%). Clearly library schools were not doing the job this group felt they should be doing.

Donna Cohen, acquisitions librarian at Rollins College, surveyed sixty accredited library schools in 1990.[12] Some fifty-two programs responded, and of these only seven had courses that were primarily devoted to acquisitions, one school did not deal with acquisitions at all, and the remaining programs deal with acquisitions as one component of a larger course topic. (As an aside, it should be noted that two of the seven programs identified above were Columbia and Brigham Young, both of which are now closed.)

The third study was an informal survey of California academic and public librarians responsible for the acquisitions function in their libraries.[13] These responses found much the same situation as Schmidt and Cohen found. Most of these respondents had no formal preparation for acquisitions work from their MLS programs. Expertise was acquired through a combination of on-the-job experience, workshops/conferences, and networking with vendors and other acquisitions librarians. Finally, when asked if acquisitions should be part of the library school curriculum, most of the respondents indicated yes, however, there was no consensus as to whether this should be through a required course or an elective course.

Finally, Pat Bril conducted a recent review of collection development oriented courses offered at the accredited library schools.[14] Bril studied the catalogs from forty-eight MLS programs (although at the time Long Island University was reworking its entire curriculum as it sought to be reaccredited), looking for collection development related courses, so it is possible that courses dealing just with acquisitions may have been omitted. She found a total of sixty-two courses offered, and then studied the course descriptions for some clue as to what subject content was actually covered in those courses and whether or not the courses were required of all students. Twenty-four of the courses were required, while the remaining thirty-eight were electives. Based on catalog descriptions, twenty-four courses cover acquisitions, however, only nine courses of this latter group of twenty-four are among the required courses. While it is impossible to discern just how much of the course is devoted to acquisitions from reading the course descriptions, Bril also included the courses titles in her survey. From this list, we find eight courses that specifically mention acquisitions in the course title. Two of these eight courses are among the required courses. It is also interesting to note that one course which includes acquisitions in the title apparently does not mention acquisitions in the content description, according to the information Bril provides.

These last four studies are interesting for a couple of reasons. First, they illustrate that over the past twelve or so years there has been little resolution to the issues addressed by the previously cited authors writing in 1978. Second, these studies further illustrate the extent to which researchers have tried to determine just how well MLS programs are preparing acquisitions librarians. You can ask the librarians, you can ask the educators, you can look at course offerings, or you can do some combination of all three, but I am not sure what kind of answers you will get. There are problems with these approaches. By asking either librarians or educators, you are dealing with subjective, impressionistic data, and that is if you can get both groups to agree on the same definition of acquisitions. Using catalogs and course descriptions would appear to be a more reliable method, however, it is far from foolproof. For example, questions of how often the course is taught, how much attention is given to individual topics (whether mentioned in the course description or not), the knowledge base of the instructor, and differences between full-time faculty and adjunct faculty can only be determined by looking at specific course material or actually observing the class in session.

THE CURRENT OUTLOOK

Where does this leave us? As I observed earlier, it has been said "Manny times, Manny weighs" that library schools are not preparing students for acquisitions work. If anything this statement is becoming more the case rather than seeing any improvement in the situation. As library schools revised their curriculums over the past thirty years, specific courses on acquisitions were found less often, and at the same time courses on collection development or technical services that were once required are now electives. Perhaps it is time for practitioners to realize that the situation in library schools is not going to change. Acquisitions is not going to play a greater role in library school curriculums than it does now as either a separate course or as part of another course. This is not to say that library schools can not play a part in preparing librarians to perform the acquisitions function. There are a number of things that can be done. First, there needs to be greater recognition of the importance of the acquisitions function, which should actually be verbalized as a greater awareness or appreciation of the business aspects of running a library. Management, marketing, and merchandising—the idea of a library as a business seems to be anathema to many people in the profession. Next, from this recognition should come greater faculty involvement in advising acquisitions as a career track, identifying relevant internship and fieldwork opportunities, encouraging independent work in the field, especially if no formal course structure introduces students to acquisitions. Finally, library schools can help plan occasional workshops and other continuing education (CE) opportunities in lieu of regular course offerings.

At the same time, the profession needs to do more than complain about library education programs and wait for them to do something. Acquisitions librarians should make faculty (and students) aware of internship opportunities. Furthermore, practitioners should be more active in sponsoring or co-sponsoring CE activities. At the end of the 1980s, ALA's Resources and Technical Services Division helped sponsor regional institutes titled "The Business of Acquisitions" (the one I am familiar with was held in Berkeley, California in April 1989). This two-day event included sessions by academic librarians, public librarians, state government librarians, publishers, and vendors.

This type of event is a good example of what practitioners can do to help themselves, although I would suggest expanding both the focus and duration of this institute. If new librarians are not learning about acquisitions in school, than an overview of the entire book trade would be worthwhile, providing the participants with an introduction to the creation and packaging of information (primarily the publishing industry, with media and electronic information included), the process of getting information packages to information users (primarily the acquisitions function), acquiring "special" materials, the financial aspects of the book trade, the impact of technology on the book trade, and other related topics. This kind of program could be run over a week-long period affiliated with a library school or run independently. Another alternative would be to offer the institute as a series of independent (but interrelated) modules as CE courses in conjunction with a conference or on a regional basis at other times, following a format similar to the Special Libraries Association's Middle Management Institute. A more thorough investigation into the possibilities of such a program may well be in order.

The last area of discussion relevant to the topic at hand deals with my earlier comments concerning the need for greater appreciation of the business aspects of running a library. If we continue to place emphasis on just the function of acquiring library materials, we will be short-changing ourselves. Libraries are very complex organizations that "acquire" many things. We acquire books, serials, technology, equipment, furniture, supplies, and people—both staff and clients. These acquisitions are worth a great deal of money, and if you begin to look at the segments of the economy that exist to service our needs as we acquire things, this economic impact becomes much greater. Yet there appears to be little awareness of this and, therefore, little discussion of this in our professional literature. However, as the way we do business changes on what seems to be a daily basis, more attention to the "business" of librarianship *will* be needed.

CONCLUSION

In conclusion, there are five points from this article to remember. First, the status of education for acquisitions has not been held in high regard in library school curriculums for some time. Second, as Schmidt, Cohen, Fisher, and Bril illustrate, that situation has not changed over the past dozen years or so. Third, there are some things library schools could do that would not necessarily impact their curriculums, but could help the current situation. Fourth, it is perhaps more important for the profession to stop waiting for the library schools and actively address some of these issues themselves. Finally, what may be necessary is a broader view of the "acquisitions" function of libraries before any of this will happen. (Of course, you should also remember the story of Manny, his watch, and his scale and use it wherever appropriate.)

REFERENCES

1. "Acquisitions Departments of Research Libraries," *ALA Bulletin* 32(October 15, 1938): 786; W. Royce Butler, "Acquisitions," *Library Journal* 91(May 1, 1966): 2271-2274; Thomas P. Fleming, "Some Unresolved Problems in Acquisitions," *ALA Bulletin* 32(October 15, 1938): 843-844.
2. William J. Myrick, "The Education of Mr. X," *Library Acquisitions: Practice & Theory* 2, 3/4 (1978): 195-198.
3. Nancy J. Williamson, "Education for Acquisitions Librarians: A State of the Art Review," *Library Acquisitions: Practice & Theory* 2, 3/4, (1978): 199-208.
4. Judith Serebnick, "Are Library Schools Educating Acquisitions Librarians?," *Library Acquisitions: Practice & Theory* 2, 3/4, (1978): 209-211.
5. Ibid., p. 209.
6. Ibid., p. 209.
7. Sara C, Heitshu, "On Formalizing Acquisitions Training," *Library Acquisitions: Practice & Theory* 2, 3/4, (1987): 205-207.
8. Joyce L. Ogburn, "Why We Need Acquisitions in the Library Science Curriculum," *Library Acquisitions: Practice & Theory* 15, 4, (1991): 478.
9. Deanna B. Marcum, "Acquisitions in the Library School Curriculum," *Library Acquisitions: Practice & Theory*, 15, 4, (1991): 471-473.
10. Ibid., p. 472.
11. Karen A. Schmidt, "The Education of the Acquisitions Librarian: A Survey of ARL Acquisitions Librarians," *Library Resources & Technical Services* 35(January 1991): 7-22.
12. Donna K. Cohen, "The Present State of Education for Acquisitions Librarianship," *Library Acquisitions: Practice & Theory* 15, 3, (1991): 359-364.
13. William Fisher, "Education for Acquisitions: An Informal Survey." *Library Acquisitions: Practice & Theory* 15, 1, (1991): 29-31.
14. Patricia Bril, Letter to the ALCTS CMDS Education for Collection Development Committee, January 21, 1993.

Advances in Serials Management

Edited by **Marcia Tuttle,** *Head,* Serials Department, University of North *Carolina--Chapel Hill* and **Jean G. Cook,** Serials Librarian, Iowa State University

Change has always been characteristic of serials, and now the nature and speed of that change have altered with the development of electronic technology. Inflation, research in preservation methods, and changes in publishers practices and vendors reservice all make their mark on serials librarianship. *Advances in Serials Management* will present essays on current issues in the topics, emphasizing response to change and clear communication among those who work up with serials as producers, processors and users.

REVIEWS: This should be considered an essential addition to general library science collections as well as those serving the needs of library science students.

-- Library Resources and Technical Services

.... a solid body of practical information of substantial value to administrators and practitioners in large libraries.

-- Wilson Library Bulletin

...this series is a welcome addition to the professional literature.

-- Library Journal

Volume 5, In preparation, Fall 1995
ISBN 1-55938-511-1   Approx. $73.25

CONTENTS: Publisher/Vendor Relations, *Ronald Akie and Mary Devlin.* Serial Linking Notes and MARC 760-787 Fields in OPAC Displays, *Joe Altimus.* Listservs within the Pantheon of Written Materials, *Sharon Dahmer.* Integratine Depository Documents Serials into Regular Serials Receiving and Cataloging Routines at the University of Oregon Library, *Karen Darling.* ISU Seminar on Scholarly Publishing, *Nancy Eaton, Bill Black, and Cindy Dobson.* A Prehistory of Electronic Journals: The EAIES and BLEND Projects, *Marilyn Geller and Bernard Naylor.* Government Publications as Serials; Serials as Government Publications, *Charles A. Seavey.*

AlsoAvailable:
Volumes 1-4 (1986-1991) $73.25 each

Advances in Library Automation and Networking

Edited by **Joe A. Hewitt,** *Associate Provost for University Libraries, University of North Carolina, Chapel Hill*

The purpose of this series is to present a broad spectrum of in-depth, analytical articles on the technical, organizational, and policy aspects of library automation and networking. The series will include detailed examinations and evaluations of particular computer applications in libraries, status surveys, and perspective papers on the implications of various computing and networking technologies for library services and management. The emphasis will be on the information and policy frameworks needed for librarians and administrators to make informed decisions related to developing or acquiring automated systems and network services with special attention to maximizing the positive effects of these technologies on library organization.

Volume 5, 1994, 282 pp. $73.25
ISBN 1-55938-510-3

Edited by **Joe Hewitt,** *Associate Provost for University Libraries, The University of North Carolina at Chapel Hill* and **Charles Bailey, Jr.** *Assistant Director for Systems, University of Houston.*

CONTENTS: Introduction, *Joe A. Hewitt.* Next-Generation Online Public Access Catalogs: Redefining Territory and Roles, *Carolyn O. Frost.* Full-Text Retrieval: Systems and Files, *Carol Tenopir.* What can The Internet Do For Libraries, *Mark H. Kibbey and Geri R. Bunker.* Electronic Document Delivery: An Overview With a Report On Experimental Agriculture Projects, *John Ulmschneider and Tracy M. Casorso.* Campus-Wide Information Systems, *Judy Hallman.* Use of A General Concept Paper As RFP For A Library System Procurement, *Mona Couts, Charles Gilreath, Joe Hewitt, and John Ulmschneider.* Research On The Distributed Electronic Library, *Denise A. Troll.* Notes on The Contributors.

Also Available:
Volumes 1-4 (1987-1991) $73.25 each

J
A
I

P
R
E
S
S

Advances in Library Administration and Organization

Edited by **Gerard B. McCabe**, *Director of Libraries, Clarion University of Pennsylvania* and **Bernard Kreissman,** *University Librarian Emeritus, University of California, Davis*

REVIEWS: "Special librarians and library managers in academic institutions should be aware of this volume and the series it initiates. Library schools and University libraries should purchase it."

-- Special Libraries

"... library schools and large academic libraries should include this volume in their collection because the articles draw upon practical situations to illustrate administrative principles."

-- Journal of Academic Librarianship

Volume 12, 1994, 282 pp. $73.25
ISBN 1-55938-846-3

CONTENTS: Introduction, *Gerard B. McCabe and Bernard Kreissman.* Ownership Or Access? A Study of Collection Development Decision Making in Libraries, *Sheila S. Intner.* A Study Of The Fit Between Theoretical Models of the Diffusion of Innovation and the Development and Diffusion of The Public Library Association's Planning Process, *Verna L. Pungitore.* Libraries, Accessibility and the American Disabilities Act, *Willie Mae O'Neal.* Some Thoughts on the Future Academic Library, *Murray S. Martin.* Library Storage: Achieving Systematic Consignments, *Cordelia W. Swinton.* Slavic and East European Librarianship Problems, Issues and Opportunities in The Post-Soviet Era, *Mark J. Bandera.* Fourth I. T. Littleton Seminar Virtual Collections: Only Keystrokes Away, *Tracey M. Casorso.* Virtual Collections: The Implications for Library Professionals and the Organization, *Sheila D. Creth.* New Technologies, Interlibrary Loan, and Commercial Services: A Symposium on the Design and Features of Electronic Document Delivery Systems, *John E. Ulmschneider.* Image-In That! Great Images Sent 'or Ere Your Pulse Beat Twice, *Marilyn Roche.* The Ohio State/Cicnet Network Fax Project: A Cooperative Library Project, *Robert J. Kalal.* NCSU Digitized Document Transmissions Project: A Summary, *Tracy M. Casorso.* Petabytes of Information: From Authors to Libraries To Readers, *Malcolm Getz.* A Model Automated Document Delivery System for Research Libraries, *John E. Ulmschneider.*

Also Available:
Volumes 1-11 (1982-1993) $73.25 each